DE HAVILLAND
AND HATFIELD
1936-1993

DE HAVILLAND AND HATFIELD

1936-1993

PHILIP BIRTLES

FONTHILL

Fonthill Media Language Policy

Fonthill Media publishes in the international English language market. One language edition is published worldwide. As there are minor differences in spelling and presentation, especially with regard to American English and British English, a policy is necessary to define which form of English to use. The Fonthill Policy is to use the form of English native to the author. Philip Birtles was born in Edgware and educated in Croydon; therefore, British English has been adopted in this publication.

Fonthill Media Limited
Fonthill Media LLC
www.fonthillmedia.com
office@fonthillmedia.com

First published in the United Kingdom and the United States of America 2020

British Library Cataloguing in Publication Data:
A catalogue record for this book is available from the British Library

Typeset in 10.5pt on 13pt Sabon
Printed and bound in England

Foreword

The de Havilland World Enterprise had grown up from being one of the world's first global manufacturing to a company with a reputation for innovative aerospace creativity, the main developments from around 1936 in a wooden semi-monocoque structure giving a strong yet light structure and a very smooth low-drag finish, which was easy to repair if damaged. Engine development continued, giving independence from other manufacturers, and propeller design continued to improve. There was an uneasy peace, but Germany was becoming a threat. Although international relations were still continuing, there were efforts to increase preparations of Britain's military. The RAF expansion plan consisting of building bomber stations was underway, with the dubious motto 'The bomber will always get through', but there was a lack of investment in defending fighters.

The company had mostly created civil aircraft since its inception after the First World War, with the occasional attempt to meet a rare military requirement during the late 1920s and early 1930s. The company made significant progress with trainers, light touring aircraft, and local service airliners, achieving great success with modern, reliable, and straightforward aircraft that could operate profitably without government subsidy. Keeping costs down was essential to penetrate the global market, where an unrivalled product support organisation had been set up with manufacturing units in Canada, Australia, New Zealand, associated companies in the USA, South Africa, and India, with licensed production set up in many other countries.

De Havilland then went on to produce the Mosquito high-speed unarmed bomber, which was adapted to many other roles, with over 7,700 produced in Britain, Canada, and Australia. Then, they went into the jet age by breaking the 'sound barrier' and producing the world's first commercial jet airliner, later developed into the Comet 4 and RAF Nimrod. Along came the take-over by the Hawker Siddeley Group as part of Hawker Siddeley Aviation, covering the development of the Trident second-generation jet airliner that pioneered automatic landing in all weathers. At this time working with the European aerospace industry, Airbus was created with Hatfield designing the high-technology wings for this highly successful family of airliners, the wings being produced at Broughton, near Chester. While the Trident was being developed, Hatfield was also busy developing the DH 125 business jet, which eventually sold over 1,800 units worldwide.

Then came the final 'DH' design, the BAe 146, by which time Hawker Siddeley Aviation had been nationalised as British Aerospace, which was later privatised. The BAe 146 was a four-engined feeder jet capable of quiet operations from short airfields such as London City Airport, bringing the passenger nearer to their desired destination. With the poor global economic situation, BAe 146 production was moved to Woodford near Manchester with Hatfield worth more as a one-off property development, which included a major campus for the University of Hertfordshire, the roots of which were de Havilland.

Now all that remains, apart from memories, is the fully restored Art Deco main administration offices and adjacent restaurant. These Grade II-listed buildings are now a Hertfordshire police headquarters, the listing being not just for the 1930s structure, but also integral with the board room and associated senior management offices where decisions were made achieving the strategic goals of the company. The Grade II*-listed aluminium structure flight test hangar also exists, and where jet airliners stood is now a fitness centre. This was listed not just for its unique structure, but also as the world's only integrated flight test facility, with aircraft hangar, control tower, fire station, offices, and laboratories capable of supporting a busy flight development operation.

The de Havilland companies produced aircraft, from trainers to supersonic jet fighters and the world's first commercial jet airliner; piston, jet, and rocket engines; propellers, guided missiles, and space rockets. These overall achievements were unequalled by any other aerospace manufacturer in the world.

This is an account based on aerospace pioneering by de Havilland and subsequent companies at Hatfield. It is not a history of the aircraft types, which are adequately covered in many other publications, but a highlight of the achievements of de Havilland since 1936 until final closure of Hatfield aerodrome in April 1994.

Philip Birtles, 2018

Contents

Foreword   5

  1   Leading Up to War   9
  2   Second World War: Mosquito   28
  3   Second World War: Vampire and Hornet   57
  4   Second World War: Supporting the War Effort   70
  5   Post-War Feederliner Developments   82
  6   Jet and Rocket Development   98
  7   Jet Fighter Developments   109
  8   Comet: The World's First Jet Airliner   124
  9   de Havilland Propellers   140
 10   Blue Streak   147
 11   DH 110 and Sea Vixen   155
 12   Comet 4   160
 13   DH 121 Trident and DH 125 Business Jet   173
 14   Airbus Wing: Centre of Excellence   201
 15   Bae 146: Britain's Most Successful Jet Airliner   207

Further Reading   224

1

Leading Up to War

With strong signs of war looming, the British Government began a serious rearmament programme in 1936, with the de Havilland companies working towards an urgent commercial aircraft policy to combat strong American competition. At the same time, they were satisfying the needs of a growing volume of design, development, manufacture, and flying training tasks, all related to the country's need for rearmament.

During this time, sport flying continued in Britain and overseas. H. F. Broadbent flew a Leopard Moth from Australia to England, achieving a record time of six days and 8.5 hours in May 1937. Major flights were made by Comet Racers with Costa Macedo, flying from Hatfield to Lisbon in 5.25 hours. Ken Waller and M. Franchonome had flown from Brussels to Leopoldville and back in 44.5 hours at the end of 1934. The race-winning Comet G-ACSS was flown by Arthur Clouston and Mrs Kirby-Green from Britain to Cape Town in November 1937 in a time of forty-five hours, with the return flight in 57.5 hours. A demanding flight in Comet Racer G-ACSS was by Arthur Clouston and Victor Ricketts in March 1938 from London (Gravesend) to Blenheim, New Zealand, and return in ten days and 21.5 hours.

The Hatfield-based Reserve Flying School, the London Aeroplane Club, and the de Havilland Aeronautical Technical School (DHATS) all contributed to the activities during this demanding period. The RAF Reserve Flying School was significantly expanded with long lines of Tiger Moth basic trainers and Hawker Hart advanced trainers on the grass outside the new school building, with a second school built at White Waltham to the same pattern and a third at Prestwick. The London Aeroplane Club was tasked with flight training of Civil Air Guard students to provide a reserve when war broke out, including ladies, many of whom joined the Air Transport Auxiliary (ATA) with wartime bases at both Hatfield and White Waltham. The Tech School improved their TK 2 racer and created the TK 4 racer in the summer of 1937, but it crashed on 1 October 1937, killing Bob Waight, the chief test pilot. Following this, Geoffrey de Havilland Jnr (the eldest son of the founder) was appointed in his place. Large orders were placed for Tiger Moth trainers for the RAF and Dominion training schemes, with additional production for in-country service in Canada, Australia, and New Zealand.

The de Havilland production process of wooden semi-monocoque construction was originally used on the DH 88 Comet Racer of 1934, the winner of the MacRobertson Air Race. The fuselage was made from a preformed birch-plywood shell with light spruce stringers, providing a light, strong, low-drag shell, the latest example being the elegant DH 90 Dragonfly, a purely civil programme. The biplane wings featured a slight sweep-back and the inner bay was kept clear of struts and wires to facilitate passenger and crew access. The wings and tail components were of traditional fabric-covered spruce construction, and heavy-duty spars were used in the wing centre section, allowing the use of a cantilever fixed undercarriage, fitted with Rapide-type nacelles with faired wheel spats; power came from a pair of de Havilland Gipsy Major engines developing up to 145 hp. There was accommodation for two pilots and three passengers in the cabin, making this one of the first executive transports. The maximum range was 900 miles with a fuel capacity of two 30-gallon tanks in the thickened lower-wing centre section, and a third 25-gallon tank in the rear of the cabin.

The maiden flight of the prototype Dragonfly A2/G-ADNA was from the grass airfield at Hatfield on 12 August 1935, followed by the first production DH 90A G-AEBU in February 1936, which was used as a sales demonstration aircraft, and was the first of sixty-six built. As was normal with new de Havilland types, the prototype was entered in the King's Cup Air Race at Hatfield on 10 July 1936, flown by Captain de Havilland and his eldest son, Geoffrey Jnr. Over the two days of the race, they averaged 143.75 mph and achieved eighth place.

The new construction methods were effective in providing excellent performance on low power, but the tooling was expensive, resulting in a selling price of £2,650, which restricted the home market to twenty-one aircraft. Among these owners were Sir Philip Sassoon, Lord Beaverbrook, and Loel Guinness. The London Aeroplane Club used G-AECW for dual instruction at a charge of £5.10s (£5.50) per hour and Air Services at Hamble used G-AEWZ as a navigation trainer. The second production aircraft (YI-HMK) was fitted out with a VIP interior for King Feisal of

Dragonfly prototype G-ADNA showing the sleek, low-drag design. (*Flight Photo*)

Iraq and was later joined by YI-OSD. Wealthy French owners Baron L. de Armella, Baron Jules de Koenigswater, Jaques Duprey, and Gustav Wolf took delivery of F-AOZC, 'YK, F-APAX, and 'DE respectively during 1936–37.

A number of airlines put Dragonflies into service, including Qantas, Wearnes Air Services, Singapore Airlines, Rhodesia and Nyasaland Airways, PLUNA of Uruguay, Divisao dos Transportes Aeros in Angola, LARES of Romania, Misr Airwork of Egypt, Ala Littoria of Italy, and the Turkish State Airline. The Swedish and Danish Air Forces both took delivery of examples. Private owners and air taxi operators ordered Dragonflies for operation in Argentine, Belgium, Holland, India, Italy, Kenya, New Zealand, Nigeria, and South Africa. The de Havilland Aircraft Company of Canada equipped CF-BFF with floats for Gold Belt Air Services, and four Dragonflies were use by the Royal Canadian Mounted Police (RCMP) to combat rum-running off the Nova Scotia coast.

Two Dragonflies had major modifications incorporated, the first probably being the prototype G-ADNA, with a large, double-curvature pilot's windscreen and canopy, as well as lowered side panels. The other was VP-KCA for Wilson Airways in Nairobi in September 1936, which had one starboard window deleted and a small freight door fitted in the side.

With an increased interest in commercial operations, a number of Dragonflies were disposed from private ownership. To add to her already large fleet of Dragons, the Hon. Mrs Victor Bruce acquired six Dragonflies at Croydon, where they were used on a contract to provide army co-operation night flying duties.

Hatfield paint shop with Dragonflies for Denmark and Sweden, a DH Dragon for Portugal, Tiger Moth for the RAF, and various civil Rapides, Dragonflys, Horney Moths, and DH 86s. (*DH Photo*)

Production ended in 1938, and in June 1940, the redundant Dragonfly jigs were used as a roadblock on the Barnet Bypass outside the factory. During the Second World War, the Royal Canadian Air Force (RCAF) took six Dragonflies, including three of the RCMP aircraft, and one was taken over by the RAAF. Fifteen Dragonflies in Britain were also impressed by the RAF to become communications aircraft, while one was retained by de Havilland for wartime communications. Repairs to the monocoque fuselage were challenging, and with spares not available, only two Dragonflies survived service use during the war, while a number of others that were not impressed survived until the 1960s. Dragonfly G-AEDU remains in flying condition in Britain at the time of writing, with another example (ZK-AYR) in New Zealand.

Following the Dragonfly was the elegant DH 91 Albatross, which was designed to provide competition with American airliners. Designed by Arthur Hagg, a contract was placed by the Air Ministry for two experimental transatlantic mail planes to Specification 36/35. The low-wing four de Havilland Gipsy 12-powered airliner used the experience of earlier types, including the Comet Racer achieving economy of operation through speed obtained by a smooth drag-reducing airframe.

The fuselage was a long, tapered circular section built with a plywood-stressed skin with layers of stabilising balsa wood in the sandwich, giving a light and strong structure. The 105-foot one-piece cantilever wing consisted of a stressed box spar with a thick spruce planking skin assembled diagonally in two layers. The main wheels were retractable into the wing ahead of the main spar. The 525-hp Gipsy 12 engines were specially designed by Maj. Frank Halford, the DH Engine Company's chief designer, by joining two Gipsy 6 engines on a common crankcase, giving a low frontal area. The specification called for a payload of 1,000 lb over 2,500 miles against a headwind of 40 mph at a cruising speed of 210 mph. The first prototype (G-AEVV) was flown for the first time by Bob Waight from Hatfield on 20 May 1937, and the aircraft was shown for the first time statically in the New Types Park at the RAF Display, Hendon, on 26 June.

Following the death of Bob Waight in the TK 4 on 1 October, Geoffrey de Havilland Jnr was appointed chief test pilot, continuing flight testing of the Albatross, early modifications to the tail configuration becoming necessary. There were also problems with the undercarriage retraction, resulting in a wheels-up landing at Hatfield on 31 March 1938. During overload take-off tests with the second prototype (G-AEVW) on 27 August 1938, the rear fuselage fractured during the final stages of the third landing run, the break being caused by the entry door opening, weakening the structure. The aircraft was repaired with reinforcing modifications and was flying again within a few weeks.

Meanwhile, five Albatrosses had been ordered by Imperial Airways with additional passenger windows fitted in the cabin, the first aircraft being delivered to Croydon Airport in October 1938 with accommodation for twenty-two passengers and four crew. The initial services were on an experimental mail service to Cairo in December, achieving an eastbound average speed of 219 mph. Regular fast schedules were then commenced from Croydon to Paris, Brussels, and Zurich from 2 January 1939. On the declaration of war, the Albatross fleet was moved to Bramcote and then Whitchurch at Bristol, where the aircraft were camouflaged for use on the Shannon to Lisbon services. The two long-range mail planes were impressed in September 1940 for service with 271 Squadron on the shuttle to Iceland, both aircraft being destroyed in crashes at Reykjavík. Of the five passenger Albatrosses, one forced landed in Gloucestershire in October 1940, the flagship was destroyed in a German raid on Whitchurch at the end of 1940, and another made a forced landing on mudflats near Shannon in July 1943. With a lack of spares, and the wooden structure delaminating, the two remaining aircraft were scrapped by the end of 1943.

Left: All-wooden
Albatross one-piece
wing production in the
Hatfield factory, 12
November 1936.
(*DH Photo*)

Below: The wooden
Albatross fuselage
being lowered on to
the one-piece wing, 16
December 1936. The
later Mosquito would
benefit from Albatross
fabrication techniques.
(*DH Photo*)

Albatross final assembly at Hatfield with five aircraft in progress and the Flamingo prototype in the background. (*DH Photo*)

Albatross final assembly and equipping, 1936. (*DH Photo*)

Queen Bee L-5902 being prepared for flight, with Albatross Prototype E.2 engine running at Hatfield, 20 May 1937. (*DH Photo*)

Three Albatross lined up at Hatfield, 29 July 1938. Mailplane prototype G-AEVV was first flown from Hatfield by Bob Waight on 20 May 1937. E-2 was the first passenger aircraft and E-3 the second mail plane. (*DH Photo*)

During overload tests, the second prototype Albatross (E.3/G-AEVW) had the fuselage fracture during the final stages of the landing run on 27 August 1938. The aircraft was repaired and strengthened within a few weeks, and back to the flight test programme. (*DH Photo*)

Albatross G-AEVV following a wheels-up landing at Hatfield on 25 March 1938 when the undercarriage failed to come down. The wooden structure suffered little damage, and the aircraft was soon back in the air. (*DH Photo*)

The three de Havilland brothers—Peter, John, and Geoffrey Jnr—in 1938. (*DH Photo*)

Following the Albatross was the one-off DH 92 Dolphin, which was an attempt to modernise the Rapide with a two-pilot side-by-side flight deck, using the experience gained with the Dragonfly structure. Power came from a pair of Gipsy 6 engines; the sole example was built in the experimental department at Hatfield, and it is only recorded as flying on 9 September 1936, followed by its final flight on 21 November. It was found to be overweight and development ceased due to the factory being fully occupied with Albatross manufacture and large-scale production of Tiger Moths for the RAF.

The DH 93 Don was an all-purpose trainer built to Spec. T.6/36, which due to no fault of the company failed to meet any of its tasks effectively. It was a three-seat low-wing monoplane with a retractable undercarriage that was powered by a Gipsy 12, which was named the Gipsy King by the Air Ministry. It used a stressed-skin wooden construction similar to the Albatross and it was fitted with dual controls for two pilots seated beside each other; the cabin provided room for radio training, and a rotatable turret was fitted for gunnery training.

The prototype (L2387) was flown from Hatfield by Geoffrey de Havilland Jnr on 18 June 1937 and was exhibited at the RAF Display at Hendon on 26 June, followed by the SBAC show the following week. The prototype was sent to the A&AEE at Martlesham Heath,

The sole prototype DH 92 Dolphin when fitted with a retractable undercarriage, which was only flown twice by Geoffrey de Havilland Jnr on 9 September 1936 and again on 21 November. It was found to be overweight and later scrapped. (*DH Photo*)

DH 93 Don general-purpose trainer under construction at Hatfield powered by a 525-hp Gipsy Twelve engine and fitted with a mock-up gun turret. (*DH Photo*)

while manufacture started at Hatfield. With Air Ministry-inspired 'improvements', the structural weight became excessive, resulting in the turret and other equipment being removed to prepare the aircraft for communications duties. The first conversion was to the third airframe and the aircraft sent to the A&AEE for service trials, allowing a small number of Dons to be issued to 24 Squadron at Hendon and a number of RAF station flights. A total of thirty Dons were completed, and a further twenty were delivered as engineless or unassembled airframes for ground instruction use with technical training schools and ATC squadrons.

The Moth family of light aircraft had been very successful, but de Havilland believed there was a market for a simple version at low cost, the new aircraft being a low wing monoplane, which was easier to produce and would have an improved performance on low power. Geoffrey de Havilland had enthusiasm for the project, which resulted in the DH 94 Moth Minor. The airframe was designed by a young team that had just graduated from the de Havilland Aeronautical School led by J. P. 'Phil' Smith—the fuselage was a proven spruce and plywood box structure, with a high aspect ratio plywood-covered mainplane using Comet and Albatross experience, with a wing fold outboard of the centre section. Major Frank Halford designed the 90-hp Gipsy Minor specifically for this aircraft, and a tailwheel undercarriage was fixed.

The prototype was first flown from Hatfield by Captain Geoffrey de Havilland on 22 June 1937, the flight test programme being shared with his son and John Cunningham. During a test of spinning with an aft centre of gravity, both Geoffrey Jnr and John had to abandon the aircraft as it could not be recovered, although once they had departed, the aircraft came out of the spin and crashed nearby. Both pilots retired to the nearby Crooked Chimney pub to await their rescuers.

By mid-1939, production rate had reached eight aircraft a week in the '94 shop' priced at £575 ex-works. Demonstration aircraft were despatched to the Australian, Canadian, Indian, and South African companies, while at home, many were ordered by domestic flying clubs taking advantage of the low cost, many being used on Civil Air Guard training. Over 100 Moth Minors had been built by the outbreak of war; however, in early 1940, production was abandoned to make room for aircraft more appropriate to the war effort, and all Moth Minor drawings, jigs. and tools, together with stocks of finished and incomplete airframes, were shipped to the de Havilland factory at Bankstown, Sydney, where at least forty were completed for the RAAF.

Many Australian Moth Minors survived the war and were demobbed to serve Australian flying clubs. A number of the British-based Moth Minors were impressed for issue to station flights, and some were fitted with coupé

Three-crew Don prototype L2387 was first flown from Hatfield on 18 June 1937, fitted with gun turret and underwing practice bombs. The aircraft was overweight and underpowered due to the general-purpose specification T.6/36 and was relegated to ground instruction. (*Flight Photo*)

Don L2390 in communications configuration was first flown on 16 August 1938 and issued to the Central Flying School at Upavon. (*DH Photo*)

Moth Minor prototype at Hatfield on 18 August 1937, having been flown for the first time by Captain de Havilland on 22 June. The second DH 71 (G-EBRV) is in the roof of the '94 Shop', but it was destroyed by enemy action on 3 October 1940. The white canteen building is in the background and still exists. (*DH Photo*)

tops over the two tandem seats, the first conversion flying in the summer of 1938. Another was fitted with a tricycle undercarriage and a canopy over the rear seat. One of the coupes (G-AFOJ) was used as a de Havilland communications aircraft during the war, joining the London Aeroplane Club at Panshanger after the war. It was flown in the South Coast and Daily Express Air Races in 1950 by Pat Fillingham, a de Havilland test pilot, averaging 137.5 mph; this aircraft still exists in non-airworthy condition. Sixteen other Moth Minors survived the war, most of which were acquired by private owners.

The first all-metal stressed-skin aircraft built by de Havilland was the DH 95 Flamingo, designed by R. E. Bishop. It was an elegant high-wing, twin-engined, local-service airliner powered by two 890-hp Bristol Perseus sleeve-valve radial engines driving three-bladed DH Hydromatic propellers. Passenger capacity was between twelve and seventeen passengers (depending upon the range required), and the crew consisted of two pilots and a radio operator. The aircraft featured split trailing-edge flaps, a retractable undercarriage, and a low-slung fuselage providing ease of loading of passengers and cargo ideal for short-haul operations. The maiden flight of the prototype was from Hatfield on 22 December 1938 by Geoffrey de Havilland Jnr and George Gibbins.

The exceptional Flamingo performance attracted the attention of the Air Ministry as a military transport within the RAF expansion scheme, the prototype being evaluated in March 1939. Commercial orders were placed by the Egyptian Government and by Guernsey and Jersey Airways, with the prototype being loaned to the latter airline in May 1939 for route-proving trials between Guernsey, Jersey, Eastleigh, and Heston; this resulted in two production aircraft being ordered. Before they could be delivered, war was declared on 3 September 1939; these two aircraft and the prototype were delivered to 24 Squadron at Hendon to be used by Winston Churchill and his advisers for trips to France before it was overrun by the Germans.

A total of sixteen Flamingos were completed—three additional aircraft for the RAF and the remainder to civil standards. The first two RAF Flamingos (R2764 and '65) were built to Spec. 21/39 for delivery to the King's Flight at Benson on 7 September 1940, and the third (R2766) was originally delivered to 24 Squadron but attached to the King's Flight during the invasion scare with the temporary civil registration G-AGCC for possible emergency use by the Royal Family. This aircraft was delivered to Benson on 7 September 1940 but went to 24 Squadron on 14 February 1941 and was joined by AE444 the following September, both aircraft being transferred to the Metropolitan Communications Squadron in September 1944. An additional military version was known

A spritely take-off of Moth Minor E.6 from the grass at Hatfield. (*Aeroplane*)

Captain de Havilland in production Moth Minor G-AFOU at Hatfield on 14 August 1939. (*DH Photo*)

DH Moth Minor prototypes at Hatfield on 3 August 1938, the middle aircraft being an early coupe conversion. In the background is the farm taken over for the aerodrome when it was established in 1930. (*DH Photo*)

The maiden flight of the Flamingo prototype was made by Geoffrey de Havilland Jnr and George Gibbins from a snowy Hatfield aerodrome on 22 December 1938. (*Flight Photo*)

The busy de Havilland production line at Hatfield with Flamingos in the foreground, and Albatross in the background, Tiger Moths, and Rapide fuselages on either side. (*Author's collection*)

The Rt Hon. Neville Chamberlain PM, arriving in France aboard Flamingo in service with 24 Squadron. (*Author's collection*)

HRH King George VI emerging from a 24 Squadron Flamingo. (*DH Photo*)

as Hertfordshire, R2510 being similar to the Flamingos, but had smaller cabin portholes. Although an order was placed for thirty production twenty-two-seat troop transports, it was later cancelled.

Seven civil Flamingos with camouflage finish were delivered to the British Overseas Airways Corporation (BOAC) at Bramcote from September 1940 to April 1941 for service in the Middle East. A further aircraft was allocated to 782 Naval Air Squadron as BT312, based at Donibristle for operations to the Orkneys, Shetlands, and Northern Ireland, which was joined by R2766 on 10 March 1945. Of BOAC fleet, three were lost in accidents, and due to the shortage of spares, all but one were taken out of service, the survivor (G-AGBY) returning home in 1944 later to be acquired by British Air Transport at Redhill.

The only Flamingo to operate after the war was G-AFYH/BT312, which was delivered to Gatwick on 19 August 1945 in Navy markings. It received a certificate of airworthiness two years later and was used for charter flying from Redhill in May 1947, but in 1949, it was stored in a hangar until May 1954 when it was scrapped due to Redhill aerodrome being closed down, although it later reopened.

Second World War: Mosquito

At the start of the Second World War in September 1939, the Hatfield factory was busy building Dominie navigation trainers, Tiger Moths, and Queen Bee target drones for the RAF, in addition to the existing Moth Minors and Flamingos. Hatfield had also taken on the production of Oxford trainers, to complement production from Airspeed at Portsmouth.

However, the company had been active with ideas about potential combat aircraft using the expertise that had been built up in the lead-up to war. As Germany became more aggressive, the de Havilland directors from 1938 were studying practical and theoretical approaches using the principle of obtaining speed through low drag designs that could be adapted for military use. Having previously been mainly involved in civil aircraft, the company was not accustomed to working with the Air Ministry, which provided the specifications for potential designs for the services.

During the summer of 1938, variations of a high-speed bomber were studied; a bomber version of the Albatross showed the most promise, with a bomb load of 6,000 lb to Berlin at 210 mph. A scaled-down version with a small-section fuselage and reduced-span wing would be adequate for the required bomb load, with a good range, operated by a crew of two, and could be fast enough not to require defensive armament. The lack of armament would save about one-sixth of the overall combat weight. As a result, de Havilland argued that leaving off the guns, gun turrets, gunners, all the extra structure, and additional fuel required would result in a smaller aircraft, which would be of similar speed to a fighter. It would be economical to build and operate, as well as be easy to maintain in the field.

The 1934 de Havilland admin. building camouflaged in 1939 in preparation for the Second World War. (*DH Photo*)

Hatfield aerodrome from the air early in the Second World War with the original farm buildings along a track from the Barnet Bypass, and the landing area disguised as fields. (*DH Photo*)

Tiger Moth production and Hurricane wing repairs with a Flamingo in the background early in the Second World War. (*DH Photo*)

Airspeed Oxford production in the Hatfield factory early in the Second World War. (*DH Photo*)

The gate house being prepared for war with sandbags. (*DH Photo*)

The camouflaged Art Deco Admin Block early in the Second World War with board room above the main entrance. (*DH Photo*)

Power would be from a pair of 1,200-hp Rolls-Royce Merlin engines. The aircraft would be made from wood, making use of the expertise already achieved with the Comet Racer and Albatross. Metal was in high demand for military use, and the aircraft would be ready a year sooner than if it was built with metal. Another advantage was the use of non-strategic labour in the woodwork industry, which otherwise would not be able to make a significant contribution to the war effort.

Following the meeting with Chamberlain and Hitler on 30 September 1938, the design team at Hatfield were clear in their minds regarding the high-speed bomber design, with Geoffrey de Havilland and Charles Walker obtaining a meeting with the Air Ministry in October to promote their ideas, the challenge being to gain acceptance as a supplier of high-performance military aircraft. All that was offered was a possibility of building wings for another manufacturer.

Following further studies and informal talks, no progress could be made until September 1939 when Germany invaded Poland, and Air Marshal Sir Wilfred Freeman, the air member for development and production, was approached with some success. Despite him being interested in the project, he experienced a great deal of opposition from the Air Council, which would normally have been daunting to most officers.

During the autumn, the design was subject to an official investigation, with discussions around the need for rear guns and gunner, but at a conference on 29 December, de Havilland was authorised to proceed with the unarmed formula. The aircraft was to have an initial overall range of 1,500 miles and be able to carry a 1,000-lb bomb load. There was also interest in using the aircraft in the reconnaissance role, and although there was no interest at the time, de Havilland promoted a long-range fighter, provisioning space under the fuselage for the rigid mounting of four 20-mm cannons. Design work went ahead with great urgency.

The design department moved to the isolated Salisbury Hall on 5 October 1939, some 4 miles from Hatfield, where the team could concentrate on the new DH 98, to become the Mosquito high-speed unarmed bomber, initially as a company-funded private venture. On 1 March 1940, a contract was placed for fifty bombers including the prototype to Spec. B.1/40, although it had not been easy to obtain agreement even for this small number, the project being referred to as 'Freeman's Folly'. The fifty aircraft were ordered straight off the drawing board, saving at least a year for service introduction.

With the defeat at Dunkirk at the end of May, the situation changed dramatically, and on 23 May, the first of many damaged Hurricanes was delivered to the factory to be repaired urgently, which required obtaining drawings from Hawker, creating repair schemes, and returning them to

Right: Captain de Havilland with a Mosquito model. (*DH Photo*)

Below: Salisbury Hall where the Mosquito was created in 1940. The prototype was hand-built in the hangar at the lowest right, closest to the hall. The hangar beyond is where the first Airspeed Horsa glider prototype was constructed. The site is now the home of the de Havilland Aircraft Museum, where the original Mosquito prototype is preserved. (*DH Photo*)

flight in support of the Battle of Britain, the Engine Company being tasked with the repair of Merlin engines. The first Hurricane was ready for flight test after only six days in the factory.

Early in June, orders came to prepare roadblocks for the Barnet Bypass along the front of the factory, and 100 old motor cars were towed in from a local scrapyard and lined up across the aerodrome as obstructions after flying finished each day, then removed the next morning.

Lord Beaverbrook was appointed minister of aircraft production as part of the new Churchill Government, with all manufacturing being concentrated on immediate operational requirements, which meant existing combat types of aircraft (many of which were totally outdated) and B.1/40 were omitted from the programmes. As a result, there was no contract cover to purchase materials, even though the demand for metal parts was very small. It was demonstrated to Lord Beaverbrook that high-strength alloy castings, almost entirely eliminating forgings, allowed the project to be reinstated in July, providing it did not interfere with the company's more important work. This included repairing Hurricanes, the production of Tiger Moth and Oxford trainers, and the fitting of bomb racks to Tiger Moths to carry eight 20-lb bombs as an anti-invasion defence. Some 1,500 sets of bomb racks were produced and issued to every flying school in Britain with instructions of how to use them at low level against invading troops. There were times when Lord Beaverbrook mentioned to Freeman that the Mosquito programme should be cancelled, but as he did not issue a firm directive, Freeman kept the project alive. It was helpful that the de Havilland team were based in the secrecy of Salisbury Hall, where the threat was not from Germany, but the Air Ministry.

To keep the Mosquito project going, a barn-like hangar was constructed across the moat at Salisbury Hall, where the Mosquito prototype was hand-built by wood and metal craftsmen, who worked six and a half days a week, including a night shift. The workers would usually travel by the no. 84 bus running between Barnet and St Albans; it must have caused some curiosity with 'farm workers' going down the drive in the dark. Although the site was never bombed, a land mine came down fairly close, and fortunately, the parachute's rigging lines caught in a tree before it hit the ground, otherwise the site would have been devastated.

In the late summer, there were further doubts about the unarmed bomber concept, but interest was beginning to be shown in a long-range fighter version, with the instruction to complete only twenty bombers, with the other thirty as fighters. However, there were still discussions whether the fighters should be single or dual control, and a gun turret was still being considered. This indecision caused inevitable delays due to three prototypes being required, with part-finished wings being strengthened and twenty-eight fuselage noses to be modified, in addition to a major increase in design work.

Every part of the company was incredibly busy. In the fifty-two days before the start of the Battle of Britain, the propeller division converted 1,051 Spitfires and Hurricanes in service from fixed two-pitch wooden propellers to the better-performing constant-speed type. Although the Battle of Britain was less intrusive in the Hatfield area, unlike the engine works at Stag Lane and the southern parts of Britain, much factory time was lost during June due to the workers taking cover whenever the sirens sounded. From 26 June, workers only went to the shelters if there was an immediate threat. Bombs fell within 1 mile of the Hatfield factory on average one day in every five throughout the autumn (the equivalent of sixty-eight bombs in 100 days), resulting in nearly a quarter of working hours lost per week, night and day, with workers in the air raid shelters.

Only once was the factory damaged—on 3 October 1940, when a low flying Ju 88 dropped four bombs from 50 feet on the wet grass, which then bounced into the 94 Shop, which was a busy sheet metal shop and the offices of the Tech School. Some workers were already in shelters, while others were on their way down the steps. The bombs killed twenty-one people and injured seventy. The building was destroyed and nine months of Mosquito work in progress was lost. This resulted in all Mosquito production being widely dispersed to avoid the catastrophic loss of work in progress. Between September 1940 and March 1941, more than one-third of the Hatfield workforce, jigs, tools, production control, and other staff had been moved into a dozen hurriedly requisitioned local premises, which were initially used for Tiger Moth and Oxford details and assemblies, with preparations made for Mosquito production to follow.

At the same time as the workforce and production was being dispersed, the subcontract department was busy locating companies to double and triplicate practically every component and assembly, and it was found that the wood-working factories in High Wycombe were practically at a standstill, with plenty of capacity and skilled labour to participate in Mosquito manufacture. To make space at Hatfield, Tiger Moth production was moved to Morris Motors at Cowley, where they were mass-produced on a moving line.

Meanwhile, work continued at Salisbury Hall on the Mosquito prototype with the ply-formed fuselage skins stabilised with balsa wood and spruce structural members and bulkheads. The bonded laminated spruce wing structure with double top skins was in one piece, with space between the inner spruce and ply ribs for the installation of fuel tanks,

Wreckage of the ''94 Shop' after the bombing of the factory on 3 October 1940. Twenty-one employees were killed, seventy were wounded, and 80 per cent of Mosquito work in progress was destroyed, resulting in production being widely dispersed. (*DH Photo*)

Mosquito bomber production at Hatfield. (*Author's collection*)

The three brothers —Peter, John, and Geoffrey Jnr—by a Mosquito tailplane. (*DH Photo*)

The founding directors in the Board Room, rear: Francis E. N. St Barbe, Wilfred Nixon; front: Charles Walker, Geoffrey de Havilland, Frank T Hearle. The chairman (Alan Butler) was absent. (*DH Photo*)

Above: Hatfield aerodrome early in the Second World War with factory buildings camouflaged as residential houses. The beacon and flying club house have been toned down. (*DH Photo*)

Left: Hatfield aerodrome and factory in 1942 with the flying area disguised with mock-painted hedgerows. (*DH Photo*)

as well as further fuel tanks in the roof of the bomb bay. The fuselage was made from two shells that were equipped with control runs down the port side and electrical cabling down the starboard side. When all the major systems had been installed, the two halves were joined along the centre line; during final assembly, the fuselage was carefully lowered over the wing, with four bolts used to hold both assemblies together. To avoid expensive machining, the main undercarriage was steel shells riveted together containing rubber in compression blocks to absorb landing loads. The radiators of the liquid-cooled Merlins were built into the wing's leading edge to reduce drag.

Having completed the prototype in its hangar at Salisbury Hall, it was then dismantled and transported to Hatfield on 3 November, and after reassembly, engine runs, and taxiing tests, Geoffrey de Havilland Jnr took E0234 for its first flight on 25 November 1940, with John Walker, the engine installation designer, as an observer. The prototype was painted yellow as an identification feature to avoid being shot at by British guns, but when on the ground outside its special hangar with a blast wall protection, it was camouflaged with tarpaulins. The aircraft had flown only eleven months since the start of design work, despite the delays caused by Air Ministry indecision. The first flight was a great success, with stunning performance and manoeuvrability; Geoffrey soon demonstrated this with upward rolls from a low level with one propeller feathered.

Preparations were in hand at Hatfield for Mosquitos to replace Oxfords, but with continued uncertainty with the go-ahead of the Mosquito, de Havilland was asked to undertake the assembly of Vickers Wellington bombers at a rate of up to 300 a month. This involved finding a new site suitable for an airfield and with adequate labour available, designing and building the factory, staffing a separate production organisation, and building up a further subcontracting organisation. This became known as the DH Second Aircraft Group and was located at Leavesden near Watford, but instead of producing Wellingtons, the factory was a second major production unit for fighter Mosquitos, largely administered from Hatfield.

Flight trials by de Havilland with the prototype, by now adopted as W4050 in January 1941, were completed in three months, proving the Mosquito was faster than any other aircraft in the world, a feature it was to maintain for the first two and a half years of the operational service. Modifications were limited to the rearward extension of the engine nacelles to cure tailplane buffet, which resulted in the wing flaps being divided, and joined by a substantial torque tube.

The all-over yellow Mosquito prototype E0234 assembled at Hatfield, camouflaged with tarpaulins. (*DH Photo*)

During trials at A&AEE Boscombe Down, where the prototype was delivered on 19 February with the top surfaces camouflaged, on 24 February, the fuselage fractured around the rear access hatch due to the rough surface of the muddy airfield. The damage was serious enough for the decision to be made to replace the fuselage with the one destined for the PR 1 prototype (W4051), which was taken from Salisbury Hall to Boscombe Down, to be changed by a de Havilland working party. During the repair process, a spruce fairing was fitted along the top of the access hatch, not only strengthening the structure, but also helping to divert rainwater from entering the rear fuselage.

W4050 returned to Hatfield on 14 March for further adjustments, including the fitting of the extended engine nacelles, returning to the A&AEE on 18 March, where it continued operational trials until 23 March. Having proved itself at Boscombe Down, despite a slow start due to lack of immediate interest, the prototype was demonstrated at Hatfield to Lord Beaverbrook and General Arnold, head of the US Air Force, with a set of drawings being sent to the USA six days later. As official interest mounted, the air minister, Sir Archibald Sinclair, visited Hatfield on 10

May with the new minister of aircraft production, Col. Moore Brabazon, when it was explained that the de Havilland companies in Canada and Australia could be allocated for Mosquito production.

On 4 May, the prototype made its 100th flight, returning to Boscombe Down where a maximum speed in level flight of 392 mph was achieved at 22,000 feet with an all-up weight (AUW) of 16,000 lb. During further handling trial at the A&AEE, the fuselage was damaged during a heavy landing where the fuselage skin fractured on the port side, just aft of the flap-trailing edge. This damage was repaired with an irregular patch on both the inside and outside of the fuselage, proving that the structure could be repaired in the field. This patch is still on the fuselage and can be seen on the prototype, where it has returned to the site where it was created in 1940 at the de Havilland Aircraft Museum. Service trials were completed with the prototype on 23 May at Boscombe Down with more representative production aircraft becoming available.

The prototype was then used by de Havilland for stall testing in a number of configurations, but in late October 1941, it was grounded for the fitting of more powerful Merlin 61 engines, flying again on 20 June 1942, reaching an altitude of 40,000 feet on the second flight. Merlin 77s were then fitted, with flight trials recommencing on 8 October, allowing the highest speed of any Mosquito at 439 mph to be achieved in November. Test flying continued at a slower rate in 1943, which included a period with Rolls-Royce at Hucknall from 1 March until 10 June. Mosquito test

HRH King George VI visiting the de Havilland factory escorted by Alan Butler (the chairman), followed by Captain de Havilland, passing employees. (*DH Photo*)

flying duties were shared between Geoffrey Jnr, his younger brother John, George Gibbins, and Pat Fillingham. On 23 August, Mosquitos HX849 and HX850, while on production test flights, collided over Hill End, near St Albans, killing John and George, plus their two observers, G. J. Carter and J. H. F. Scrope.

In December 1943, the prototype was grounded to be used for apprentice training. It was exhibited publicly at the SBAC displays at Radlett in September 1946 and 1947, where it was surrounded by a selection of the typical weapons loads; it was struck off charge as Cat. E on 21 June 1947, going into storage at various de Havilland locations, where it was hidden by Bill Baird, who resisted instructions to burn W4050. It was allocated to Salisbury Hall in a specifically constructed Robin hangar, where the museum opened to the public for the first time on 15 May 1959, the first aviation museum in Britain. It is now fully restored in the configuration when it last flew.

Meanwhile, at Salisbury Hall, the fighter prototype W4052 was ready to fly, armed with four fixed, forward-firing 20-mm cannons and 0.303-inch machine guns in the nose. To save a month of dismantling and reassembly, Fred Plumb asked Geoffrey Jnr to take a look at the field near the hangar. It was downhill sloping and only 450 yards long, but with a light load, Geoffrey decided to make the flight with Fred Plumb as a passenger on 15 May 1941. Two days before, a German courier, Karl Richter, had parachuted into a field just over 1 mile from Salisbury Hall but was caught the next day and executed at Wandsworth on 10 December.

During the winter of 1940–41, de Havilland was instructed to convert twenty of the bombers to the photo-reconnaissance role, which was fortunately the same basic configuration as the bomber, but then an instruction came through to finish ten of them as bombers after all.

The first fully equipped bomber prototype (W4057) was completed in the experimental department at Hatfield, and after company flight trials, it was delivered to Boscombe Down on 27 September 1941, followed by the first production B.I on 18 October; both were returned to Hatfield to be adapted to carry four 500-lb bombs.

The first delivery was made to the RAF in July 1941 when PR Is arrived with to the Photo Reconnaissance Unit (PRU) at Benson, with six on strength by September, the initial sortie being by W4055 on 17 September.

The main bomber development was B Mk IV powered by Merlin 21 or 23 engines, developing 1,460 hp each, and could carry four 500-lb bombs internally, by clipping the vanes with no change in ballistics performance. When two-stage Merlin 61s were fitted, the aircraft became

Captain de Havilland's youngest son, John, in a Mosquito cockpit. He was killed with three other crew members in a Mosquito mid-air collision on 23 August 1943. (*DH Photo*)

the B Mk IX, replacing earlier versions on the Hatfield production line in March 1943. A number of B Mk IVs were converted to carry a pair of Barnes Wallis-developed 'Highball' mines recessed in tandem in the bomb bay for use as anti-shipping weapons by 618 Squadron. 'Highball' was a smaller version of 'Upkeep' used by 617 Squadron in the dams raid.

A major development was the B Mk XVI, which was the Mk IX fitted with a pressure cabin for high-altitude operations, and the bomb-bay was enlarged by fitting new bulged doors to accommodate a single 4,000-lb 'Cookie' bomb. This brought the Mosquito bomb load to the equivalent of the USAAF B-17 Flying Fortress, an all-metal slower aircraft with four engines and a crew of up to ten. A high-speed unarmed Mosquito (with a crew of two and powered by two Merlins) could operate to Berlin twice a night with a very low loss rate of less than 1 per cent. The final bomber version was the B.35, the initial one making its first flight on 12 March 1945, powered by a pair of 1,609-hp Merlin 113/114s, giving a top speed of 422 mph at 30,000 feet, but it did not enter service until after the end of the war. During the 1950s, a number of surplus Mk 35s were adapted as TT.35s for target towing.

The photo-reconnaissance development followed very much along the lines of unarmed bombers, carrying cameras and additional fuel tanks in the converted bomb bay, the PR IV being fitted with two-stage Merlin XXIs giving an improved high-altitude performance and improved crew comfort with the later addition of a pressure cabin. As an interim, ninety PR IXs were built at Hatfield between May and November 1943, powered by a pair of 1,680-hp Merlin 72/73s with an 18-lb boost, increasing the range to 1,500 miles. The prototype PR XVI first flew in July 1943, achieving 40,000 feet. The PR 32 was a reduced all-up weight version, with extended wingtips for sustained operation at 40,000 feet in an attempt to keep clear of enemy jet fighters. The ultimate PR 34 was similar to the B.35 but with additional fuel tanks in the enlarged bomb bay, allowing very long endurance for operations particularly in Asia, although this version did not enter service until after the end of the war.

Mosquito B.IVs and FB.VIs were used by BOAC in civilian markings for a high-speed courier service between Leuchars in Scotland and Stockholm in neutral Sweden, known as the 'Ball Bearing' run. Being neutral, Sweden was allowed to trade with both sides, but Britain successfully negotiated to take the full production ball bearing capability of Sweden, denying any to Germany. In addition to up to half a ton of payload, these Mosquitos would also carry important passengers, reclining in the enclosed bomb bay on a mattress with oxygen. Although it was a flatbed, it was not quite business class. The 800 miles were flown in around two and a half hours, bypassing 300 miles of occupied Denmark and Norway, from which German fighters would attempt to intercept them.

The Mosquito fighter differed in the configuration of the fuselage, with the bomb aimer's transparent nose replaced by four 0.303-inch machine guns, and under the forward fuselage were installed four 20-mm cannons. This required moving the crew entry door to the side of the forward fuselage. The bomber 'Vee' windscreen was replaced by a toughened, laminated, flat windscreen resistant to gunfire. The cannon breaches projected back into the front part of the bomb bay.

The original contract was for the completion of fifty bombers, but on 18 July 1940, de Havilland received an instruction to build a fighter, and the third airframe (W4052) was completed to Spec. F.18/40 as the night fighter prototype. The gun turret was still being considered, with the four nose-mounted machine guns moved to a turret mounted behind the canopy and occupied by a third crew member. Although it involved very little increase in weight, the drag of the installation was unacceptable, reducing both the top speed and range.

Two prototypes (W4053 and W4073) were allocated to turret trials and assembled at Salisbury Hall, making a total of four Mosquitos completed at this location. Mosquito W4053 was flown out of the fields adjacent to Salisbury Hall on 14 September, but by the time the aircraft had landed at Hatfield, pieces of the turret had become detached. W4073 was flown out of Salisbury Hall by George Gibbins on 5 December, but this was only fitted with a mock-up turret, which was removed soon after.

In January 1941, a further change was to modify twenty-eight bombers to the fighter configuration, and the overall matt black fighter prototype (W4052) was delivered to Boscombe Down for service trials on 23 June, fitted with an early version of AI radar with the antenna mounted between the nose-mounted machine guns.

The first airborne trials were against a target RAF Blenheim on 5 September, and the Mosquito design was so free from drag that the pilot had difficulty slowing down for interceptions and a Youngman frill-type airbrake was fitted around the rear fuselage aft of the wing trailing edge. In the event, it was found that it was just as effective to use the flaps to slow down, avoiding the weight and complication of the airbrake. The matt black was found to reduce the speed by 10 per cent, the equivalent of 26 mph, resulting in a replacement by the standard day camouflage. During the flight development programme, problems were found with the flutter of the original fabric-covered elevators, particularly with the original short engine nacelles, so they were skinned with aluminium.

In July 1941, the company was ordered to build Mosquitos in large numbers in Britain and Canada, with engineers going to Canada to organise production and adapt the design to local materials and equipment. There was a major expansion at Hatfield with the addition of 400 subcontractors, including several large furniture manufacturers and engineering companies all over Britain, from major concerns to small cycle manufacturers, and including groups of neighbourly housewives. With 800 Oxfords completed at Hatfield during 1941, transfer of production to other factories had to be organised. Leavesden and its dispersed units completed 140 sets of Oxford components, plus sixty fuselages and 147 wings, followed by Mosquito wings and fuselage shells for assembly at Hatfield, before being allocated to full Mosquito production.

Like any powerful twin-engined aircraft, the Mosquito was capable of flying on one engine, but ease of control was reduced. On Sunday, 9 April 1942, Geoffrey Jnr was flying in W4052 at 20,000 feet over Bedford when the port engine began to vibrate. He shut down the faulty engine as a precaution, and with plenty of height available, he decided to return to Hatfield. Due to there being no radio communications with air traffic, when Geoffrey was committed to land, a departing Proctor, whose pilot had no knowledge of the emergency, took off in the path of the Mosquito. Geoffrey therefore was forced to overshoot and struggled over Welwyn Garden City at low speed, while attempting to raise the undercarriage and flaps without losing lift. Fortunately, he spotted the ex-decoy airfield of Panshanger, which was used by the de Havilland-operated elementary flying school. He made a wheels-up landing on the grass; the aircraft jacked up the next day, ready for repair, and was flown back to Hatfield on 5 May, demonstrating the light damage of wooden structure and ease of repair. On 29 May, Geoffrey made another wheels-up landing, this time at Hatfield, when the undercarriage of B.IV DK291 failed to lower.

To indicate the preparedness of de Havilland at Hatfield, the design and production team were always ready to adapt the Mosquito for urgent special requirements. On 5 September 1942, a Ju 86P high-altitude reconnaissance aircraft flew over Hatfield, but being above 40,000 feet, it could not be pursued. Two days later, de Havilland was asked to produce a one-off special high-altitude Mosquito fighter. In seven days, the prototype pressure cabin bomber MP469 was converted into a four-cannon fighter with an increased wingspan, smaller wheels, a reduced fuel capacity, and less armour, saving 2,300 lb of weight. The change of configuration was made simply by sawing off the bomber nose and scarfing on a fighter nose, a process that could not have been done with a metal aircraft. John de Havilland managed to reach 43,500 feet, but the Ju 86Ps flew over fairly rarely for a few months, eventually stopping altogether. Five B Mk IV Mosquitos were similarly converted to carry AI Mk VIII radar and a four-cannon armament pack was located under the fuselage as the NF XV.

Hatfield became the focus of attention in early 1943, when the enemy plan was to sabotage the factory power supply, disrupting Mosquito production. The saboteur selected was double agent Eddie Chapman, who had been imprisoned in Jersey for robbing safes, when the Germans took over occupation. After much persuasion, Chapman convinced the Germans that he would work for them in return for his freedom. He went through a rigorous training programme, winning the trust and confidence of his masters. However, the British secret service was aware of his plans to return to Britain through intercepted radio traffic, but his capture had to be undercover; otherwise, the interception of radio traffic would be compromised. On his initial parachute landing in East Anglia, he contacted the Ely police, from where he was taken to London to be

Mr Eric Gander Dower with his new Dragon Rapide at Hatfield on 29 July 1942 with camouflaged aerodrome beacon in the background. (*DH Photo*)

Dominie Mk I X7524 at Hatfield on 1 September 1942. (*DH Photo*)

The camouflaged Hatfield factory and aerodrome in 1944. (*DH Photo*)

Mosquito night fighter prototype W4052 after a wheels-up landing at Panshanger by Geoffrey de Havilland Jnr on 9 April 1942. (*DH Photo*)

Mosquito Mk XV MP469 rapidly modified from a bomber airframe with a Vee-windscreen and lower crew entry door, with a four 0.303-inch machine gun nose spliced on. The aircraft was reduced in weight, wing span was increased, and four-blade propellers were fitted for high-altitude operations against high-flying Luftwaffe reconnaissance bombers. (*DH Photo*)

interrogated by the secret service, when he revealed all he knew about German espionage methods. Due to the high value of this information, M15 was persuaded that he could become a double agent, with the codename Agent Zig-Zag.

Masterman of M15 decided that Chapman should demonstrate his sabotage skills to the enemy as soon as possible, and the de Havilland factory at Hatfield was selected for a large-scale staged explosion, the results of which would be reported in the newspapers. Chapman therefore made a reconnaissance of Hatfield as if he really was going to sabotage the factory, so when he was debriefed by the Germans, he would have an accurate account. He walked around the aerodrome, where he saw some Mosquitos dispersed, and then went to the main gate, where he could see the power generating plant just inside on the left.

With the knowledge of the de Havilland management, Chapman and his secret service minder returned that evening, entering the factory to inspect where the four large transformers were located, so that he could devise a practical plan for their destruction, bringing production to a halt. The quantity of explosives required was more than one person could carry, so an accomplice was invented, and Chapman was taken shopping for the explosive ingredients, to test the possibility of his destruction plan, obtaining the materials from high street shops.

Camouflaged 'damage' to the powerhouse by Agent Zig-Zag: Eddie Chapman, 30 January 1943. (*DH Photo*)

To simulate the damage would take the expertise of a camouflage expert, and a magician called Jasper Maskelyne was brought in to simulate the damage caused by a very large explosion in the power plant. Pieces of damaged generators were laid out around the site with rubble and debris scattered about, and the existing generators were camouflaged to indicate a large hole in the ground, where the generators should have been.

The night of 29–30 January was chosen for the event, when there was expected to be clear skies, and the moonlight would allow the conjuror's team to do the set-up. A German photo-reconnaissance aircraft was allowed to fly overhead unmolested to record the damage. In addition, the editor of *The Times* had to be briefed, but the editor refused to print the bogus news as it was against the principles of the newspaper. However, the editor of the *Daily Express* had no such scruples and agreed to print the story in the early editions, which was passed to the German consulate in Lisbon. The controlled explosion went off just after midnight, which was heard by many of the Hatfield residents, and the results were so convincing that Chapman gained great credibility with his German masters.

As a postscript, Chapman moved to Shenley Lodge on Ridge Hill just south of Salisbury Hall, and he and his wife were guests to events at what is now the de Havilland Aircraft Museum, where the author was a trustee. Eddie Chapman died at the age of eighty-three on 11 December 1997.

Probably the most effective Mosquito development was the FB.VI, which combined the offensive armament of the fighter with the bomb-carrying capability of the bomber. Based on the fighter airframe, the AI radar was removed and a smaller bomb bay due to the breach blocks of the cannons taking up space at the forward end resulted in only two 500-lb bombs being carried internally. The load was made up by carrying a pair of 500-lb bombs on underwing pylons on what had become the universal wing fitted to all Mosquito variants, capable of carrying any armament cleared for use on the aircraft and easing production variations. This version was optimised for ground attack and took over the hazardous task of low-level precision attacks against heavily defended targets, including enemy shipping. The FB.VI was also capable of carrying eight underwing 60-lb rocket projectiles (RP), which in a maritime attack was the equivalent of a broadside from a cruiser. The FB.VI continued in production for the remainder of the war, the type being built at Hatfield, Leavesden, and mass-produced by Standard Motors at Coventry, making it the most numerous Mosquito version produced. It was also interesting that after the war many of the senior management cars were Standard Vanguards.

The only major development of the FB.VI was the Mk XVIII, adapted for maritime duties against German U-boats in the Bay of Biscay, with the 20-mm cannons replaced by a single adapted anti-tank 57-mm 6-lb shell Molins cannon. There was concern that the structure would be unable to absorb the recoil effect of the gun, but in practice it was better than metal structure. Initial trial firings were made at the Hatfield gun butts from early June 1943, followed by service trials at Boscombe Down from 12 June. Due to the specialist role, only a small number of FB XVIIIs were produced and were operated by a detachment of 618 Squadron based at Predannack in Cornwall from 24 October 1943.

The major fighter development of the fighter Mosquito was for night defence, which was powered progressively by more powerful Merlin engines and equipped with improvements in AI radar as it became available. With the fitting of more effective radar, the nose-mounted machine guns were replaced by a radome, an electronically transparent protection for the rotating scanner. The first 'thimble' radome-housing AI Mk VII was installed in Mosquito DD715 in July 1942, and following successful trials at the Royal Radar Establishment (RRE) at Defford, authority was given for ninety-seven Mk IIs to be delivered from the Leavesden production line to Marshall of Cambridge for radomes to be fitted, commencing on 2 January 1943, with the aircraft then being flown to Defford for the installation of the highly classified radar systems. The aircraft were designated NF Mk XII with initial deliveries to 85 Squadron at Hunsdon in Hertfordshire on 28 February ready for combat. The NF XIII was a conversion of the FB VI airframe powered by Merlin 21 or 23 engines and increased fuel capacity from 547 to 716 gallons to give greater endurance.

A new universal radome was developed to accommodate both British and American radars, which were being developed in parallel, and the NF XIX, powered by more powerful Merlin 25s, was fitted with the first of 2,000 American AI SCR720 radars in January 1943, the initial aircraft being DZ659. A further ninety-eight Mk IIs were delivered from Leavesden to Marshall for conversion and fitting the American radar to become the NF XVII. Meanwhile, the first NF XIX was delivered to Ford on 1 April, only eight weeks after the conversion had started.

In April 1944, the NF 30 was developed from the Mk XIX by fitting a pair of two-stage Merlin 72s, the initial example being MM686. After solving problems with the exhaust shrouds, this version entered service in late 1944, becoming a great success with Fighter Command, 100 Group, and the 8th USAAF. The final RAF night fighter was the post-war NF 36 with more powerful Merlin 113s and improvements to the radar. The ultimate night fighter Mosquito was the NF 38 with further improved radar, but it was not adopted by the RAF, with the majority of the production going to the emerging Yugoslav Air Force, and a NF 38 was the last Mosquito to be built when it was completed at the Broughton factory, named after the local village, near Chester. Aircraft were flown from the adjacent Hawarden (pronounced Harden) airfield, which was also the base of 48 MU RAF, where many of the subsequent Vampires and Venoms were delivered simply by towing them across the airfield to be prepared for service or temporarily stored.

Although too late to see combat service, the Sea Mosquito was developed for the Fleet Air Arm (FAA), some with manually folding wings and capable of carrying a torpedo externally. Captain Eric 'Winkle' Brown made the first deck landing at sea in the world by a twin-engined aircraft with Mosquito FB.VI LR359 aboard HMS *Indefatigable* on 25 March 1944.

The parent company was responsible for the support and training for all Mosquito operations, with the service and spares department at Hatfield assessing repair schemes after accidents or combat damage. A Mosquito Repair Organisation was set up at Hatfield, with additional resources being gained from industry and RAF maintenance units (MUs). To understand the scale of the undertaking, one in every four Mosquitos delivered for operational service during the war came from the repair depots. The home organisation delivered 2,074 Mosquitos up to 15

Mosquito NF.XIX fitted with nose-mounted radome over AI Mk VIII radar, for the Royal Swedish Air Force. These aircraft were modified by Fairey at Ringway and are seen ready for delivery from Hatfield on 26 February 1949. (*DH Photo*)

The last Mosquito (NF.38 VX916) at Broughton on 15 November 1950, with the workers involved in its production and test flying. (*DH Photo*)

August 1945, of which 1,252 were repaired by de Havilland. In addition, de Havilland incorporated major modifications in 1,131 Mosquitos, with DH field engineers modifying 3,847 aircraft at operational units. The Hatfield-based salvage unit reduced 357 Mosquitos beyond repair to vital spare parts. Every Mosquito unit in the RAF and USAAF in Britain, Europe, the Mediterranean, India, Burma, Asia, and North America had a DH representative attached, providing support and organising working parties to keep Mosquitos in the air. This worldwide product support was to form the basis of the global airliner support in peacetime.

The First and Second Aircraft Groups at Hatfield and Leavesden delivered a total of 4,444 Mosquitos up to August 1945, with Standard Motors at Coventry building 1,066 FB.VIs, Percival Aircraft at Luton 198, mainly PR versions, and Airspeed completed twelve bombers. In addition to 1,750 Tiger Moths and 375 Ansons, DH Canada built a total 1,134 Mosquitos. In Australia, 212 Mosquitos were produced. With post-war production, including at Broughton near Chester, 7,659 Mosquitos were built worldwide, with Hatfield making 3,349 and Leavesden 1,566.

The Mosquito was therefore the original multi-role combat aircraft, serving as an unarmed bomber, unarmed low and high-altitude photo-reconnaissance, long-range fighter and intruder, night fighter, pathfinder, naval strike, courier, target tug, and trainer. When it first flew, it was 20 mph faster than the Spitfire, powered by the same engine and with twice the wetted area. With an overall loss rate of around 1 per cent, the crews were able to survive due to its high-speed, small frontal area, and high manoeuvrability, whereas the RAF and USAAF heavy bomber losses were sometimes over 10 per cent on a raid, which in the long term was unsustainable.

The salvage hangar of the Mosquito Repair Organisation, 18 May 1944. (*DH Photo*)

The Mosquito flight line outside the flying school hangar with a B Mk XVI in the foreground and fighters behind, 15 February 1944. (*DH Photo*)

The last Hatfield-built Mosquito B.35 (TK656) rolled out on 10 April 1946 and delivered to the RAF on 12 May 1946. (*DH Photo*)

Sir Geoffrey de Havilland in his office in November 1954, knighted in 1944 for services to aviation. (*DH Photo*)

3

Second World War:
Vampire and Hornet

The Hornet was the ultimate in propeller-driven high-speed fighter, and the Vampire was de Havilland Aircraft's first jet aircraft, powered by a de Havilland Goblin engine.

In early 1941, before major Mosquito production was fully launched, consideration was being given to entering the jet propulsion field with discussions between the de Havilland aircraft and engine design teams. Major Frank Halford had started the design concepts of a turbojet in the same year, resulting in the aircraft project being designated the DH 100. However, it was still too early to put the aircraft company design team on to a jet aircraft before the engine had been clearly defined.

Therefore, by the autumn of 1941, senior members of the design team began looking at a twin-engined night bomber powered by Halford-designed Napier Sabres, using Mosquito experience. In October, this was proposed as the DH 101 and was so well received by the Ministry of Aircraft Production that it was given priority over the jet fighter, with a possibility of later developing the DH 101 into a twin-jet bomber. With preliminary design work proceeding, in April 1942, it was found that due to other priorities, Sabre engines would not be available for the DH 101, which was abandoned. Consideration was then given to a lower-powered night bomber powered by a pair of Rolls-Royce Griffons, with a payload of around 5,000 lb at a slower speed than the Mosquito. Instructions were to proceed in April with what was designated the DH 102, but in early May 1942, permission was granted to proceed with the jet fighter, powered by the Halford H.1, later to become the Goblin, which had been running on the testbed at Hatfield since 13 April.

By September 1942, construction of the jet fighter mock-up was well advanced in the experimental department at Hatfield, with the cockpit layout established, and the twin-boom tail configuration had been mounted in position on the engine testbed to ensure there was adequate clearance for the jet efflux. A twin-boom layout for the jet fighter was chosen to maintain a short jet pipe to avoid losses in thrust due to friction with a long jet pipe. However, design work was slowed as there was a renewed interest in the Sabre bomber, but with the development problems of Sabres for the Hawker Typhoon, a better option appeared to be a long-range fighter powered by Merlins for the expected campaign against the Japanese.

In November 1942, de Havilland management sought the advice of Sir Wilfred Freeman, who was by then vice chief of the air staff, with the responsibility of co-ordinating research with production. He advised pressing on with the jet fighter project, to settle many unknowns about the concept, and there was no other project to feature Halford's new turbine. It was proposed that the night bomber be dropped and proceed with the twin Merlin long-range fighter, an advantage being the design of the jet fighter could be finished off quickly, to be followed by what had become known as the DH 103. In December 1942, the DH 102 night bomber was dropped, with full pressure on the jet fighter; by January 1943, the mock-up of the DH 103 was making progress, and it was the only project using a new very promising high-performance Merlin. Full approval for the DH 103 was not instant, as the Ministry was busy with many projects, with work on the DH 103 suspended until June, when it also received the full go-ahead.

The DH 100 prototype was ordered to Air Ministry Spec. E.6/41 and initially known by the codename 'Spider Crab'. Although the specification called for an experimental prototype, the design team made provision for four fixed 20-mm Hispano cannons in the underside of the fuselage. The new jet fighter was to be designed and built at Hatfield, but the production facilities were saturated with Mosquito production, resulting in Vampire manufacture being undertaken elsewhere. The official specification called for a maximum speed of 490 mph and a service ceiling of 48,000 feet. To achieve this performance using a new form of power, and armed with four guns requiring 150 rounds each, required a very efficient low drag design. What was to become the de Havilland Vampire was the last unsophisticated fighter to be flown by the RAF, combining simplicity with jet performance.

Three prototypes were built in the experimental department at Hatfield, the smooth, streamlined fuselage nacelle being constructed from a plywood and balsa wood sandwich over moulds as with the Mosquito. The fuselage was made in two halves, each one being equipped before joining along the centre line. The single pilot was housed in a forward-located cockpit with a rearward-sliding bubble cockpit canopy (but no ejection seat), with the

Prototype Vampire LZ548/G, codenamed 'Spider Crab', at Hatfield a month before its first flight by Geoffrey de Havilland Jnr on 20 September 1943.

pilot having an excellent unobstructed view, particularly on the ground. The fabric-covered fuselage pod up to the engine bulkhead had a smooth finish, and the remainder of the structure was flush-riveted aluminium construction, with easy access all around the jet engine using wrap-around cowlings. Simplicity was maintained with all flying controls being manual, and no radar fitted, the gun aiming being by a simple gyro gunsight. As there was no need for propeller clearance, the tricycle undercarriage was short, making access easy without ground steps, the pilot climbing aboard using recessed steps in the fuselage side.

The Vampire prototype (LZ548/G) was flown off the grass at Hatfield for the first time by Geoffrey de Havilland Jnr on 29 September 1943, only sixteen months after detailed design was commenced, and by early 1944, it was exceeding 500 mph by a handsome margin over a wide-altitude range. The first prototype featured tall fins and rudders, but production versions had a flat top fin and rudder, later adapted to the familiar curved DH configuration. The wings featured an equal taper on the leading and trailing edges, and there was provision for underwing jettisonable fuel tanks to help extend endurance. The second and third prototypes (LZ551/G and MP838/G) soon joined the flight development programme, the third aircraft being fitted with four 20-mm cannons.

The initial order for production Vampires was for 120 aircraft, later increased to 300, with the English Electric factories at Preston undertaking final assembly at Samlesbury. The first production F Mk 1 (TG274/G)

Second prototype Vampire (LZ551/G) fitted with an arrester hook for carrier trials.
(*MOD*)

made its maiden flight on 20 April 1945, with the first sixteen aircraft joining the flight development programme at Hatfield and government establishments. The first prototype took no further part in the programme after it was destroyed following an engine failure on take-off from Hatfield on 23 July 1945, with de Havilland test pilot Geoffrey Pike escaping without serious injury.

The second prototype was given a 4 per cent increase in flap area, lengthened undercarriage oleos, and an arrester hook for deck trials on HMS *Ocean*, becoming the first jet aircraft to land on a carrier on 3 December 1945 when flown by Capt Eric 'Winkle' Brown. Before flying on and off the carrier, mock deck trials were made at Farnborough by flying into an arrester wire at various speeds and offset distances. As a result of the hook breaking, the supports were strengthened to reduce on-board ship hazards. Further practice on land was made on 2 December at RNAS Ford, ready for the actual deck trials the following day. Despite poor weather, 'Winkle' Brown located HMS *Ocean*, and preparations were made for the first landing, with the most demanding feature of the approach being making the decision to abort any landing early, due to the slow acceleration of the early Goblin engines. Once established on the approach, it was possible to see the ship pitching and rolling more violently than expected.

However, the batsman gave excellent guidance, bringing the aircraft straight down to a gentle landing, despite the tail-skids hitting the deck just before touch-down. The aircraft was soon refuelled and made an unassisted take-off, which was so short it was 20 feet up when passing the captain's lookout on the bridge. On the fourth landing, the flaps were damaged by the arrester wires, but by removing 4 sq. feet of area, the trials continued three days later. Despite the trial's success, Vampires did not enter combat service with the FAA, partly due to the poor acceleration of the Goblin engine in the event of an overshoot, and the lack of endurance over a hostile sea where a number of approaches may be required in poor weather. Some Vampires saw service with the FAA, but as advanced trainers.

Meanwhile, the third prototype powered by a 2,500-lb thrust Halford H1A engine was delivered to the A&AEE at Farnborough for service trials in April 1944, where the overall impressions were favourable, but there was a poor rate of climb and slow acceleration caused by the engine being in an early stage of development. The second production Vampire was converted to a Vampire F.3 to Spec. F.3/47 powered by a Goblin 2 developing 3,100 lb thrust; the forty-first and subsequent Vampire off the Samlesbury production line were built to the same standard. Pressurised cockpits were fitted from the fifty-first production aircraft (TG336), and the earlier canopy was replaced by a one-piece unit from TG386 in January 1946.

TG276 was the first of four Vampire F Mk 2s built to Spec. F.11/45 powered by a Rolls-Royce Nene turbojet developing 4,500-lb thrust, which was delivered to France as a Mistral development, the French licence-built version of the Vampire. The fourth Mk 2 was shipped to

First deck landing by a jet fighter by Capt Eric 'Winkle' Brown on HMS *Ocean* 3 December 1945 with Vampire prototype LZ551/G. (*DH Photo*)

Australia to become the prototype of the F.30, to be licence-built for the RAAF. Vampires were too late for service in the Second World War, with initial deliveries to 247 Squadron at Odiham in April 1946, followed by 54 and 130 Squadrons in October. There were enough Vampires with 247 Squadron to participate in the Victory Day flypast over London on 8 June 1946, the first time they had been seen in public.

The third production Vampire (TG278) with a 4-foot extension to each wingtip and a special pressure canopy, powered by a 4,400-lb thrust Ghost turbojet, was used for high-altitude trials of the engine, during the course of which John Cunningham established a new world altitude record of 59,446 feet on 23 March 1948, taking off and landing back at Hatfield.

The next development for the RAF was the Vampire FB Mk 5 which had the wingspan reduced from 40 feet to 38 feet, to optimise it for low-level ground attack. The wing was strengthened for the carriage of bombs or RP, the first production example flying on 23 June 1948, the type being used in Asia against Malayan terrorists, as well as serving widely with the 2nd TAF in Germany. The final RAF development was the Vampire FB Mk 9 optimised for operations in the tropics, and when the last was delivered in December 1953, Vampire totals for the RAF were 1,157 aircraft. Production had been at Samlesbury, Broughton, and Fairey Aviation at Ringway.

Vampires were also popular with many overseas air forces, one example going to Canada as a pattern aircraft for local production. The first export order came from Switzerland, who ordered four Mk 1s for evaluation, followed by seventy-five FB Mk 6s, the export version of the FB 5, many of which were assembled at Hatfield. This was followed by Sweden who ordered 70 Mk 1s, with further examples going to Egypt, Finland, Iraq, Lebanon, Norway, Venezuela, India, South Africa, Italy, and New Zealand, in addition to developments in Australia, France, and Canada. A total of some 3,269 Vampires were built in Britain, with a further 1,097 overseas.

The DH 103 Hornet was a scaled-down version of the Mosquito, using the same construction process, but for the first-time bonding metal to wood on the top wing double skin with wood on the outer layer and aluminium on the inner layer, using the specially developed Redux bonding. To achieve the greatest efficiency for the longest endurance, the aircraft was designed with attention to low drag, and Rolls-Royce designed special Merlin 130/131s developing 2,070 hp, which were enclosed in low frontal area cowlings. The engines powered de Havilland four-blade propellers, and to counter the swing on take-off due to the high power, the propellers rotated in opposite directions. A mock-up was constructed in the experimental department and first viewed by representatives from the Ministry of Aircraft Production in January 1943. Permission was given

The initial pair of evaluation Vampire F.1s for the Swiss Air Force ready for delivery on 27 July 1946. Geoffrey de Havilland Jnr is fourth from the left and John Cunningham is wearing the trilby hat on the right. Some of the Propeller Company test fleet is on the other side of the aerodrome. (*DH Photo*)

Swiss Vampires and civil Doves in production at Hatfield on 16 February 1949. (*DH Photo*)

Early Royal Swedish Air Force Vampires ready for delivery from Hatfield on 4 June 1946 with Mosquitos and Hornets in the background. (*DH Photo*)

Geoffrey de Havilland Jnr by Vampire F.1 TG278 at Hatfield on 20 September 1945. (*DH Photo*)

Vampires were sold widely for export, an example being Venezuelan 2-A36 seen at Hatfield near the watch office ready for delivery on 20 December 1949. (*DH Photo*)

the following June for the programme to go ahead, and Spec. F.12/43 was written around it.

Although looking similar to the Mosquito in layout, it was a completely new design, with the slim oval section wooden fuselage being moulded over concrete moulds. The one-piece, two-spar, cantilever laminar flow mainplane was designed to high strength factors with a composite wood and metal internal structure, a stressed birch ply/aluminium double upper skin, and a reinforced Alclad undersurface. The pilot sat in a bubble canopy covered cockpit in the nose giving excellent all-round visibility, and the main armament was four fixed 20-mm cannons mounted under the nose. Later provision was made for underwing bombs for use in the ground attack role.

The prototype (RR915) was flown for the first time from Hatfield by Geoffrey de Havilland Jnr on 28 July 1944, only thirteen months after the start of detail design. The predicted performance was exceeded handsomely, the prototype achieving 485 mph, which was faster than any other production propeller-driven aircraft. During the first sixty days of flight development shared by Geoffrey Jnr and Geoffrey Pike, 50.5 hours were flown. The second prototype (RR919) was completed fitted with a pair of 200-gallon drop tanks under the wings, giving a range of over 2,500 miles when cruising at 340 mph at 30,000 feet. It was while flight testing these large underwing fuel tanks that Geoffrey Pike had engine problems. He attempted to drop the fuel tanks, but one failed to release, and he was forced to abandon the out of control aircraft, resulting in it crashing in a cottage garden at Barkway, Hertfordshire.

Hornet prototype RR915 taxiing from the Experimental department for first flight on 28 July 1944. (*DH Photo*)

The first production Hornet F Mk 1 for the RAF (PX210) was delivered to Boscombe Down on 28 February 1945, but the war with Japan was over before any could be delivered for service with the RAF. An alternative role for the Hornet in Asia was photo-reconnaissance, and three prototypes of the PR Mk 2 were built fitted with rear fuselage-mounted cameras, followed by five production PR 2s before the order was cancelled. Improvements to the Hornet resulted in the F Mk 3, the first of which was PX312, fitted with wider tailplane, large elevator horn balances, and provision for 200-gallon fuel tanks under the wings, which could be replaced by a pair of 1,000-lb bombs. Internal fuel tankage was increased from 360 to 540 gallons, giving a 40 per cent increase in range.

Production was at Hatfield until late 1948, when the jigs were moved to the Broughton factory, with the first off the line there flying in March 1949. From here, the total numbers reached 211 Hornets, with completion in June 1952. The F Mk 3s were all fitted with a curved dorsal fin to improve high-speed stability. The first RAF unit was 64 Squadron at Horsham St Faith near Norwich from February 1946 with F.1s, F.3s arriving in April 1948, and Hornets also equipping 19, 41, and 65 Squadrons. All Hornet F.1s were declared obsolete by the RAF in 1950, and most of the F.3s were sent to Malaya for the Far East Air Force (FEAF) fitted with underwing rails for eight RP against terrorists in the jungle, becoming the last piston-engined fighter to see RAF service. The last twelve aircraft built were the F Mk 4 fitted with one vertical F.52 camera.

The other major version of the DH 103 was the Sea Hornet for the FAA. During the early DH 103 studies, a carrier-based version was considered against the Japanese, which with high drag flaps and counter-rotating engines made it ideal for deck operations. In late 1944, three production F.1s were selected for naval modifications to Spec. N.5/44, with design work allocated to Heston Aircraft, who produced a wing with power-folding as well as other naval features. Airdraulic undercarriage legs replaced the basic rubber in compression design, to absorb the higher rate of descent on to the deck. The first two prototypes were standard hooked Hornets without folding wings, but the third prototype fitted with folding wings commenced deck trials on HMS *Ocean* on 2 October 1945. A production order was placed for the FAA first twin-engined long-range escort fighter, designated Sea Hornet F Mk 20, with the first example flying from Hatfield on 13 August 1946, joining 703 NAS at Lee-on-Solent for service trials. The naval version was armed similarly to the RAF Aircraft with four 20-mm cannons, and the carriage of two 1,000-lb bombs or eight 60-lb RP under the wings, with camera station in the rear fuselage. Sea Hornet F.20s entered service with 801 NAS at Ford on 1 June 1947, remaining in front-line service until 1951 with production ceasing in June of the same year.

There was also an urgent naval requirement for a high-speed night fighter, which was achieved by modifying the Sea Hornet F.20 into a radar-equipped two-seat NF 21, with Heston Aircraft again responsible for the design to Spec. N21/45. ASH radar was fitted in the nose, with the second crew member in an enclosed cockpit on the fuselage top behind the wing trailing edge. The prototype conversion first flew on 9 July 1946, and despite the additional drag, the F.21 was only 5 mph slower than the previous versions. Deck trials started on HMS *Illustrious* on 25 October 1948 and production commenced at Hatfield, until the jigs were moved to Broughton at the end of 1948.

Out of a total of 198 of all types of Sea Hornets built, seventy-eight were NF 21s. The only front line unit to operate the NF 21 was 809 NAS, which reformed with the type at Culdrose on 20 January 1949. Forty-three Sea Hornet PR 22s fitted with two F.52 cameras were also operated by the FAA, and after withdrawal from service most of the Sea Hornets were scrapped at Yeovilton in 1956.

Hornet F.3 PX393 SH-W of 64 Squadron with the opposite rotation of the propellers shown. (*DH Photo*)

An unconventional arrival on Hatfield aerodrome with Hornet F.1 PX315 when the concrete runway was being constructed. (*DH Photo*)

Pat Fillingham flying Sea Hornet F.20 TT202. He was responsible for the majority of Hornet and Sea Hornet flight development. (*Aeroplane Photo*)

Sea Hornet NF.21 VZ697 of 809 NAS about to catch the arrester wire. It features a pair of RP rails and drop fuel tank fairings under each wing. (*RNAS Lossiemouth Photo*)

4

Second World War: Supporting the War Effort

Not only did de Havilland produce three outstanding combat aircraft during the Second World War, but there were also many other ways the war effort was supported. Tiger Moth production had already been moved to Morris Motors at Cowley, followed by the Dominies, production of which was moved to the Brush Coachworks at Loughborough in 1943. Some 200 examples were built at Hatfield before the move, and a further 275 were completed by Brush by 15 August 1945.

Perhaps the most important development with the Engine Division was the creation of the Goblin turbojet. The de Havilland Engine Division was headed by Major Frank Halford, who had served with the Royal Flying Corps (RFC) in the First World War. He was recalled to use his engineering talents on aero engine development. In 1922, he took part in the Senior TT on a Triumph Ricardo motorcycle, finishing in thirteenth place. In 1923, he set up his own consultancy, where, working with Captain Geoffrey de Havilland, he developed the long line of Gipsy air-cooled inline family of engines. From 1928, Halford worked for Napier, developing the powerful Sabre 'H' layout engine, which was used in the Hawker Typhoon and Tempest fighters.

During the Second World War, he began to develop a turbojet engine; when the de Havilland Engine Company was formed in 1944, his consultancy was absorbed, and he became managing director and chief engineer. Halford was in discussions with Sir Henry Tizard, who encouraged turbojet development, but not only was Halford busy with other projects, the de Havilland Engine Division had traditionally been involved with the Gipsy range of engines, and the design team had been widely scattered to other locations with priories in the factories for mass production. Following discussions with Charles Walker, de Havilland chief engineer, and the Hatfield design team were ready to look at designing a 500-mph jet fighter, the decision being reached in early 1941. This resulted in de Havilland being recognised as the first turbojet engine builder in Britain with a quantity production capability.

With a high level of security and only a small number of engineers, the design of the Halford H.1, later the Goblin, commenced, under the codename of 'Supercharger', the first detail drawings being issued for manufacture on 8 August 1941. New turbojet engine facilities had to be created from scratch, with considerable support from the Government, the project requiring a new approach to thermal, dynamic, mechanical, and manufacturing considerations, including the use of special metals to cope with the high temperatures and stresses.

On 13 April 1942, 248 days after the issue of drawings, the prototype turbojet was started for the first time on the specially built testbed at Hatfield, with an armed guard surrounding the building. Two days later, a thirty-minute acceptance test was run at half speed, the subsequent stripping down, showing no problems. The engine was then reassembled and the development running programme started, ready for the first official visit by the Jet Collaboration Committee, with the chairman, Dr Roxbee Cox, responsible for coordinating companies and government departments working on gas turbines. They saw the jet running on 2 May.

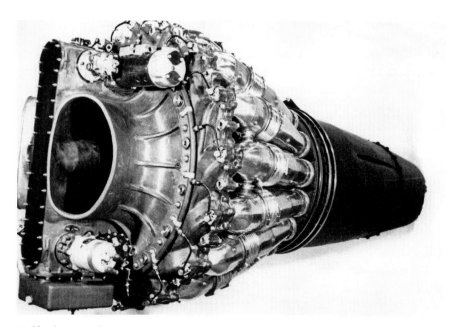

Halford H.1 turbojet engine, 18 January 1942. (*DH Photo*)

By this time, its characteristic whine could be heard from the aircraft side of the aerodrome, bringing many enquiries from visitors to de Havilland, the explanation being given that it was a new electrical plant.

On 5 May, the engine seized and stopped due to the intake ducting being sucked flat by the impeller, which required a complete strip down to check for damage. Fortunately, little damage resulted on this occasion and the engine was run at full speed on 2 June for the first time, demonstrating its design thrust within two months of starting runs. By 25 July, de Havilland was instructed to investigate production arrangements, and on 10 September, they were requested to submit a complete plan for manufacture, which by working around the clock was achieved on 18 September. A completely new factory arrangement, with building work and new machine tools were set up at Leavesden. On 26 September, the two-hour flight approval run was completed, by which time bench running had reached nearly 200 hours with two engines, and others were close to starting.

Although the basic design of the H.1 changed little, it was a characteristic that performance could be improved significantly by small improvements in efficiency. A compressor was used to simulate the forward flow of air in flight conditions, and by early 1943 the efficiency of the Goblin compressor was measured. Following some two years of design and testing, the new jet engine was ready to power an aircraft in flight, but the Vampire was not ready due to preoccupation with Mosquito and Hornet development. However, as the Rolls-Royce Welland turbojets were not ready for the twin-jet Gloster Meteor prototype first flight, a pair of H.1s was supplied to allow Michael Daunt to make the first flight on 5 March 1943. Geoffrey de Havilland Jnr took the Goblin-powered Vampire aloft for the first time on 20 September.

The Americans were kept informed of turbojet developments in Britain and with some thirteen hours of flight testing on the Vampire, the first of a few Goblins was shipped on 30 October 1943 to Lockheed in California, to power their new XP 80A Shooting Star fighter prototype, which flew for the first time in January 1944 and soon achieved 500 mph. Thus, the first aircraft to exceed 500 mph in Britain and America were powered by the de Havilland Goblin. It became the first jet engine to pass the Air Ministry type approval tests in January 1945, by which time the new factory was in full production to provide power for successive versions of the Vampire.

On 1 February 1944, the de Havilland Engine Company was formed, with Frank Halford as the technical head and chairman of the board. Aubrey Burke was director and general manager, Brodie was director in charge of the engineering division, and Dr Moult was chief engineer. The new company was formed during the busiest year of the war, with the Allied

Meteor prototype DG206 made its first flight powered by a pair of Halford H.1 engines. (*DH Photo*)

Goblin turbojet engine on a test stand, 13 November 1944. (*DH Photo*)

invasion of France. While being a separate company, the Aircraft Company was one of its best customers, the two organisations working closely together, with Halford also a director of the parent company, confirming a working relationship going back thirty years to the DH 4. Although the main jet engine production facilities were at Leavesden, engine testbeds were set up on the far side of Hatfield aerodrome, later expanding into the very comprehensive Halford laboratory engine testing facility.

In 1934, de Havilland acquired a licence to manufacture variable pitch propellers from Hamilton Standard in America, with manufacture commencing in 1935, preparing for eventual war design, development, and production, a capability that otherwise did not exist. It was also the start of the de Havilland Propeller Division, with works initially at Stag Lane, later expanding into a major wartime mass-production factory at Lostock, near Bolton in Lancashire. This allowed the DH factories to produce over 100,000 propellers, the major share of all variable pitch propellers for the RAF and Fleet Air Arm during the war. In addition, a further 37,801 propellers were assembled from parts made in America, and 40,708 propellers that had been damaged in service were repaired.

By the time of the fall of Paris to German advances, de Havilland had delivered around 1,250 two-speed propellers for Hurricanes, 1,000 for

Turning off a Goblin turbojet after completing 500 hours testbed running on 27 August 1948. *Left to right*: unknown RAF officer, Aubrey Burke, Frank Halford, Dr Eric Moult, Hugh Buckingham, Brodie, and unknown technician. (*DH Photo*)

Spitfires, and 325 for Defiants. Constant speed propellers were already being delivered in quantity (mainly for the bombers), with about 5,000 supplied. During the Battle of France, de Havilland engineers and test pilots were hearing from fighter pilots that the Luftwaffe Bf 109s had a higher ceiling than our fighters, although their manoeuvrability was not so good. They also had an advantage accelerating in a power dive, while the RAF two-pitch propellers had to be throttled back to avoid over-revving. It was agreed that constant speed propellers would be much more effective, which did not need the propellers to be replaced, but only governors and piping to be fitted.

On Sunday 9 June, with the German armies advancing rapidly across France, a RAF engineering officer contacted de Havilland, requesting the conversion of one Spitfire as an example. A test pilot and engineer were sent to explain the work required, which would not take long to achieve, but if there was a requirement to make quantity modifications, authority would be needed to divert materials and labour from the existing demanding contracts. Work started to assemble the parts for the trial installation, which were ready in four days, and six DH engineers completed the conversion in one night at an RAF airfield. In a report dated 20 June, the DH test pilot confirmed that he had flown the converted Spitfire, as well as Sqn Ldr Cook (the commanding officer of 65 Squadron) and a number of his pilots. It was estimated that the absolute ceiling was increased by 7,000 feet, with improved manoeuvrability at height, in addition to reduced take-off run and increased rate of climb.

As a result, on 22 June, a verbal instruction came to de Havilland for the conversion of all Spitfires, followed by Hurricanes and Defiants to be converted in the field. Conversions commenced at twelve fighter stations, starting on 20 July, de Havilland having begun the manufacture of 500 conversion sets without contract cover, with a rate of production of twenty sets a day from 24 June. In addition to the field modification kits, Supermarine was supplied with twenty sets per week for aircraft coming off the production line, resulting in two-thirds of production being with constant speed propellers. When DH engineers had completed the squadron aircraft, all the aircraft in storage at maintenance units (MUs) were also modified.

Day and night raids on England began on Monday 24 June, and the next day, thirteen DH engineers set out for the twelve designated Spitfire stations, each carrying six conversion kits to get started. Some of the squadrons resting after the rigours of Battle of France and Dunkirk flew their Spitfires from South Wales and the north of England in ones and twos to have their aircraft converted; some were flown into Hatfield for conversion. By Friday 2 August, forty-four days after the first test flight of the Spitfire, the production sets for all existing Spitfires was complete, with more going to the Supermarine production line. Work then started on 400 Hurricane conversions, with the total eventually being 700, after which all new aircraft would have the modifications embodied on the production lines. The bulk of the work was completed six days before the major Luftwaffe attacks commenced.

By 16 August 1,051 Spitfires and Hurricanes had been converted, an average of 20.2 aircraft per day over fifty-two days. In eight days between 8 and 15 August, German losses averaged eighty-one aircraft daily, four times the RAF losses. One of the senior officers in Fighter Command remarked to a DH engineer that without the conversion to variable pitch propellers, the figures may have been reversed.

The major material used in propeller construction was duralumin, despite worries about metal shortages. With regard to ease, cheapness and accuracy of manufacture, plus ease of repair and handling, longevity, top speed, and cruise, the 'dural' blades were ideal. With developments in strain gauging, blade design improved and weight was reduced. Propeller repair was a vital source of units, with the repaired propellers output sometimes exceeding new production. Blade ductility allowed propellers damaged in crashes to be repaired many times, and the two main repair depots in Britain returned some 40,000 propellers to service during the war.

As part of the training programme for pilots, 13 E&RFTS was based at White Waltham, near Maidenhead, and opened by de Havilland on 16 November 1935 as the base for the second flying school providing *ab initio* flying training mainly on Tiger Moths, with Hart advanced trainers and Ansons for twin-engined training. The administrative HQ was a replica of the 'Art Deco' school at Hatfield. Up to 3 September 1939, some sixty pilots had been trained.

The site was bombed on 3 July 1940 by a Do 17 killing one and injuring six other personnel. Six Tiger Moths were destroyed, and a further twenty-five were damaged. On 20 December 1940, 13 EFTS was moved to Westwood, Peterborough, and it became the HQ, main operating base, and training school for the Air Transport Auxiliary (ATA). The new organisation commenced operations on 15 February 1940 when No. 3 Ferry Pilots Pool, equipped with Tiger Moths and Magisters, formed with forty pilots. The aim of the ATA was to train relatively experienced pilots, many of them ladies, who were not able to qualify for combat, to ferry new aircraft from the factories to squadrons without disrupting operations. These pilots could fly anything from a Spitfire fighter to Lancaster bomber single-handed in all weathers. The ferry pilots pool was equipped with Ansons, Arguses, and Dominies, to collect the ATA pilots

Martin Baker MB.5 R2496 fitted with a six blade de Havilland contra-rotating propeller at Hatfield, 18 November 1947. (*DH Photo*)

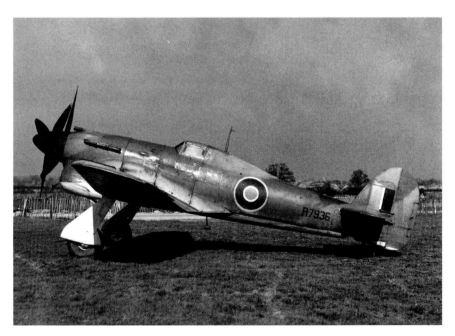

Sole Rolls-Royce Vulture-powered Hawker Tornado prototype R7936, built by Avro and first flown from Langley on 31 August 1941, later used by de Havilland Propellers at Hatfield as a testbed for six blade contra-rotating propellers. (*DH Photo*)

from the delivery point and return them to base for the next delivery. The ATA made 308,567 aircraft delivery flights during the Second World War, and there was another ATA women's section based at Hatfield from January 1940, which concentrated on the delivery of Mosquitos from Hatfield and Leavesden. Amy Johnson was one of the ferry pilots, who on 5 January 1941 had departed Squires Gate at Blackpool for Kidlington in an Oxford; she became lost in bad weather and crashed in the Thames Estuary, drowning before she could be rescued. The ATA group moved to Luton on 1 April 1942, eventually disbanding on 18 May 1943.

On 8 June 1940, Hatfield became an operational RAF station with the arrival of 2 Squadron's Lysanders as part of the overall anti-invasion strategic plan, and they were joined by Lysanders of 239 Squadron on 18 September 1940. No. 2 Squadron moved out to Sawbridgeworth on 24 October 1940, followed by the departure of 239 Squadron on 22 January 1941. On 17 February, Lysanders of 116 Squadron arrived but left after a short stay on 24 April 1941. Tiger Moths and Harts of 1 EFTS moved to nearby Panshanger on 7 September 1942 to reduce congestion at Hatfield.

The peak of training capacity was in the middle of 1941, when the school had forty-two instructors, ninety Tiger Moths, and 180 pupils, one of the flights already having been dispersed to Panshanger. A total of 43,700 flying hours were achieved in 1941. Panshanger had started life in 1940 as a decoy airfield with buildings made from film sets, complete with dummy aircraft and cars, the eventual airfield being located close to the decoy site.

The de Havilland Aeronautical School, of which the author was an engineering student, was started in 1928 at Stag Lane, moving gradually to Hatfield from 1934. Initially, apprenticeships had to pay for their training, but de Havilland pioneered the introduction of Dr Barnado's persons as free entries, many of them serving for many years with the company at all levels. In the first months of the war, there was a rush of apprentices and instructors to join the forces, leaving the school somewhat depleted in numbers.

In the bombing of 3 October, most of the school records were destroyed, one instructor was badly injured, two apprentices were killed, and several more injured. From 1941, the school began to expand with R. W. Reeve as the new principal, and indentured apprentices were exempt from military service until the age of twenty, resulting in the training courses being condensed into three years. Following basic training (including fitting; sheet metal; woodworking, including making a toolbox; milling; and turning), the apprentices—both craft and engineers—would be allocated to the various shops and departments in the factory for practical training. A hostel was established nearby at Sherrards, Welwyn, and Salisbury Hall

Two ATA female pilots at Hatfield on 22 October 1941 with Oxford AT652. (*DH Photo*)

A group of eight ATA female pilots at Hatfield by ferry Dominie. (*DH Photo*)

Hatfield Polytechnic (originally Hatfield Technical College and now part of the Campus of the University of Hertfordshire) was built on land donated by Alan Butler, chairman of the de Havilland Aircraft Company. It was originally opened in 1952 and provided the theoretical standards for students of the de Havilland Aeronautical School. (*Author's collection*)

Astwick Manor was taken over by the de Havilland Aeronautical School in 1948, when moved from Salisbury Hall. The Manor was used for student accommodation for their first year and the Airspeed hangar moved from Salisbury Hall was used for initial practical training. (*DH Photo*)

was the headquarters after the school was bombed, by which time the Mosquito team had returned to Hatfield. By the end of the war, the school had trained nearly 700 engineering and trade apprentices. In total, ninety-six engineering apprentices joined the forces during the war, and fourteen were killed. Forty-eight trade apprentices joined up, three of whom lost their lives. After the end of the war, the Tech School expanded significantly under Reeve, with 2,000–3,000 apprentices in the engineering and trade categories, with degree courses at universities and further education at Hatfield Technical College, later to become the University of Hertfordshire. The original land for the College was purchased by de Havilland and presented by Alan Butler, the company chairman. Bob Reeve retired on 31 May 1959.

The de Havilland companies had contributed an enormous amount of effort during the Second World War, with directly employed people rising from 5,000 to 38,000 over seven years, with tens of thousands more working for sub-contractors. In the year 1936, before expansion commenced, the turnover was around £1.4 million, rising to £25 million in the last year of the war, not including government shadow factories or associated de Havilland companies overseas. Large numbers of women were employed throughout the company, rising to between 30 and 40 per cent of the total labour force. Executives worked a seven-day week, with a day off when advisable. There was no discrimination between management and employee, allowing talent to be recognised for an apprentice to maybe become a director, many of the senior managers having started in the Tech School, a process that continued after the end of the war.

5

Post-War Feederliner Developments

During the Second World War, the Allies agreed that while Britain forged ahead with development and production of combat aircraft, America would also work on the development of transports, producing the Douglas DC-4 and Lockheed Constellation, both of which would be produced into fine commercial airliners with the end of the war, with no competition from Britain. From early 1943, with a growing confidence of Germany losing the war, thoughts were being considered on what Britain could produce in terms of competitive airliners to American types in different classes. With Britain's lead in jet propulsion, R. M. Clarkson had been studying civil applications for jet propulsion, with details passed to Captain de Havilland, who was one of the aviation industry members of the Second Brabazon Committee, tasked with considering aircraft categories required after the war. Headed by Lord Brabazon of Tara, a jet-powered mail carrier was one of the categories considered, with another being a piston-engined medium-sized airliner as a potential DC-3 replacement, resulting later in the Airspeed Ambassador.

A third category was for a light transport with a capacity for about eight passengers as a modern replacement for the pre-war Dragon Rapide, powered by two of the new range of six-cylinder Gipsy 70 supercharged engines driving DH Hydromatic propellers. It would be an all-metal low-wing monoplane that could be readily available after the war with a potentially large global market, and not subject to political considerations. Following consultations with the overseas DH companies in Canada, Australia, South Africa, New Zealand, and India, it was confirmed that there was a high level of support two years before the war ended, allowing design and construction of the Dove to commence during the latter part of 1944.

With the end of the Second World War, the de Havilland Admin Block was returned to its former glory. (*DH Photo*)

Meanwhile, as an interim measure, de Havilland was directed by the government several months before the collapse of Germany to make available some of the war surplus production of Dragon Rapides to civil operators both in Britain and overseas as soon as possible after the war ended. One of the first airlines to adopt the Rapides for commercial service was KLM, which began to operate PH-RAA from Amsterdam in September 1945. By February 1946, more than 100 Rapides had been sold worldwide for around the equivalent of £6,000, including services in Europe, Middle East, Africa, Canada South America, and Australia. The civil conversions were generally made at the de Havilland airfield at Witney, Oxfordshire.

Designed by a team led by R. E. Bishop, who had led the Mosquito programme, what was to become the Dove was designed to the Brabazon Type 5B requirement and built to Air Ministry Spec. 26/43. The all-metal semi-monoque fuselage was fitted with two-piece cantilever wings, with the main spar passing through the passenger cabin. A pneumatically retracted nose wheel undercarriage was fitted, with good visibility for two crew from the flight deck. It featured for the first time the specially Ciba Geigy-developed Redux metal-to-metal bonding, saving structural weight and giving a reduced drag finish. The prototype (G-AGPJ) was hand-built in the experimental department at Hatfield and was flown for the first time by Geoffrey Pike on 25 September 1945, only six weeks after the defeat of Japan, and also the twenty-fifth anniversary of the founding of the company. This was the first of over 500 Doves built at Hatfield and Broughton from 1951 for operators worldwide.

Despite a considerably improved performance over the Rapide, many of the charter airlines were unable to recover the higher initial purchase price and 50 per cent greater operating costs, resulting in early deliveries being to airlines in Africa, the Middle East, India, and Asia. One Dove was converted to a float configuration be DH Canada in 1947, and others were sold to companies for business use in North, Central, and South America, with Argentina taking delivery of seventy Doves. British-based airlines included Skyways, Hunting, Olley, and Morton Air Services, the latter two based at Croydon Airport. The Civil Aviation Flying Unit (CAFU) had a fleet of Doves for calibrating and checking airfield radio aids and testing commercial pilot candidates. The Dove Mk 1 in the airline configuration could typically carry eight passengers, but the high-density layout was eleven passengers by leaving out the toilet in the rear entrance vestibule. At Hatfield, the rear vestibule area was known as 'the loo with a view' as with the window removed, the Dove was used as an air-to-air photographic mount. The Dove 2 was the business version with a six-seat executive interior introduced in 1948 with examples sold widely to major companies in Britain as well as overseas.

The Dove 3 was a projected high-altitude survey version but was not built. The forty-eighth production aircraft was ordered to Spec. C.13/46 as the Dove 4 for military communications transport. Cabin seating was reduced to seven, with the forward starboard seat replaced by a 'J' type dinghy. An initial batch of 30 was ordered by the RAF as Devon C Mk 1 serving with the Metropolitan Communications Squadron at Hendon, headquarters communications flights, and some major overseas embassies for the use of air attaches. Devons were also sold to air forces in the Middle East, Africa, India, Pakistan, and New Zealand. In 1955, ten mainly civil Doves were converted to military configuration as Sea Devon C Mk 20s for operation with the FAA, including 781 NAS, with three more added in January 1956. The Dove 5s and 6s were similar to the earlier Mk 1s and 2s, but with 380-hp Gipsy Queen 70 Mk 2s increasing the all-up weight (AUW) to 8,000 lb, which was equivalent to a 20 per cent increase in payload over a 1,500-mile stage. Many of the earlier Doves were fitted with the more powerful engines during major overhauls.

The ultimate de Havilland version of the Dove was the Mk 8 re-engine with a pair of 400-hp Gipsy Queen 70 Mk 3s, with larger oil cooler intakes above the spinners and exhaust thrust augmenter tubes under the engines to reduce drag. The most obvious airframe change was the installation of

Dove prototype G-AGPJ was flown for the first time on 25 September 1945, the twenty-fifth anniversary of the formation of de Havilland Aircraft Company. After early flight trials, it was fitted with an interim dorsal fillet, parked on the experimental apron on 27 November 1945. (*DH Photo*)

West African Airways Dove VR-NAB ready for delivery from Hatfield on 25 August 1947, with the concrete runway being constructed in the background. (*DH Photo*)

Olley Air Service Dove G-AJOT by Croydon Airport's iconic terminal building and control tower on 1 October 1947. (*DH Photo*)

Float equipped Canadian Dove CF-DJH flying over Toronto on 26 September 1947. (*DH Photo*)

VIP Devon C.20 XJ324 781 NAS 'Admiral's Barge' at Northolt on 7 July 1970. (*Author's collection*)

a Heron style higher profile flight deck fairing. The first Dove 8 (G-APYE) was first flown in February 1960, and demonstrator G-ARDH was exhibited at the Farnborough Air Show in the following September, with the first delivery (G-ARJB 'Exporter') to J. C. Bamford Excavators on 24 January 1961. The Dove 7 was similar to the Mk 8 but used for passenger transport. In 1965, eight RAF Devons were re-engined to Dove 8 standard, later receiving the modified canopies to become Devon C Mk 2s.

In America, Riley Aeronautics replaced the Gipsy Queen engines with 400-hp Lycomings with an improved flight deck and restyled interior as the first stage, the second stage including a sweptback fin. At least seventeen were converted in the USA, and McAlpine Aviation at Luton converted a small number for domestic use, one of which had the swept fin.

An enlarged development of the Dove was considered in 1945, but the market did not exist at the time, and it was not until 1949 that detail design commenced under the leadership of W. A. Tamblin. Emphasis was on rugged simplicity for economic operations on short to medium stages in areas where there were no properly developed aerodromes. The nose wheel undercarriage was fixed, and the four engines were ungeared, unsupercharged, reliable 250-hp Gipsy Queen 30s with an already well-established long overhaul life. The engines drove two-blade DH variable pitch airscrews, giving an exceptional small field performance. The new fourteen-seat aircraft was built in the experimental department at Hatfield using Dove outer wings and an extended Dove fuselage, as well as Dove

A rare occasion when the HSA corporate Dove 8 fleet were gathered at Hatfield on 15 November 1977, consisting of G-AREA (Hatfield), G-ARHW (Woodford), G-ARBE (Brough), and G-ASMG (Dunsfold). (*Author's collection*)

Above: McAlpine Aviation Dove Turbo 400 G-ATGI at Luton on 14 March 1972, powered by a pair of Lycoming 10-720 engines and fitted with a toilet compartment behind the entrance vestibule with an additional window. (*Author's collection*)

Below: Full Riley Dove-conversion N1472V visited Hatfield on 20 November 1964, powered by Lycoming engines and a swept-back fin and rudder. (*Author's collection*)

nose and tail units. The first prototype (G-ALZL) was flown from Hatfield by Geoffrey Pike on 10 May 1950. During the first 180 hours of test flying, the original tailplane was changed to one with dihedral.

The first production aircraft went to New Zealand National Airways, which left Hatfield on 2 April 1952 on its delivery flight. Only seven Herons were built at Hatfield before production was transferred to Broughton; the last of the seven (G-AMTS) was the first Heron Mk 2 with a retractable undercarriage, making its first flight on 14 December 1952. Without the drag of the fixed undercarriage, cruising speed increased by 20 mph, and it had improved fuel consumption, replacing the Mk 1s on the production line. Production continued at a slow rate, the 143rd Heron being completed at Broughton in May 1961. The type served in thirty countries, with some being used for business transports, including three to the Queen's Flight at Benson from May 1958. In May 1961, the Royal Navy replaced five Sea Devons with ex-civil Heron 2s, which were delivered to Lee-on-Solent as Sea Heron C.20s and used as 'admiral's barges'.

Some Herons had their Gipsies replaced by Lycoming engines in the USA, known as Riley conversions, with improved performance and higher load-carrying capability. A more extensive remanufacturing programme was by Saunders Aircraft in Canada, who replaced the four Gipsy Queens with two United Aircraft PT-6A-27 propeller turbines, the first conversion flying on 18 May 1969.

Since it first opened in 1930, Hatfield aerodrome had grass surface runways, but with plans for the development of a jet airliner, it was decided to construct a single 2,000-yard concrete runway, 24/06 (magnetic runway headings) in the direction of the prevailing wind with connecting perimeter track providing access from both sides of the airfield. This new feature came into use on 12 May 1947.

A major decision was taken on 27 April 1946, when the Propeller Division was formed into a separate company—de Havilland Propellers—to give this part of the company some degree of autonomy, similar to the Engine Company. A new factory and administrative offices were constructed at Hatfield on the north side of the aerodrome along what was Manor Road. There were two hangars available to accommodate the flight testing of propellers and equipment. The new company pioneered the first propeller in the world to achieve type approval for the use in a gas turbine installation, the first reverse pitch propeller for braking an aircraft after landing, and the first manually variable-pitch propeller type approval to benefit light aircraft.

The Engine Company was busy supplying Gipsy Queens for Dove sales and Goblin engines to support Vampire production. By early 1946, Gipsy production had moved from Stag Lane to Leavesden, and for a time, Goblin production was at Stone Grove in Edgware near Stag Lane.

Heron Series 1 prototype G-ALZL under construction in the Experimental Department at Hatfield on 31 January 1950 by second Comet prototype. (*DH Photo*)

Heron Series 1 prototype G-ALZL pushed out of the Experimental Department on 10 May 1950, ready for Geoffrey Pike to make the first flight the same day. (*DH Photo*)

Three Herons of the Queen's Flight in-formation on 29 April 1958. XM295 and XM296 are C Mk 4s and the farthest away is C Mk 3 XH375 used by HRH the Duke of Edinburgh. (*DH Photo*)

Saunders ST-27-stretched Heron CF-XOK powered by a pair of PT-6 turbine engines visited Hatfield on 22 July 1971. (*Author's collection*)

The new concrete runway—on compass headings 24/06 was laid for the Comet flight testing, with the threshold of a grass runway—32 leading across. (*DH Photo*)

Hatfield aerodrome with the new concrete 2,000-yard runway in the early 1950s with the flight test hangar in use, and the de Havilland Propeller Company flight test hangars on the Manor Road side. (*DH Photo*)

Engine design and development continued on the 14-acre site at Stag Lane, while testbeds and flight test were located at Hatfield. A larger development of the Goblin was the more powerful Ghost, design of which had started during the latter part of the war; it made its first test run on the Hatfield testbeds on Sunday, 2 September 1945, to become the engine for Venom developments, also developed for use on the new jet airliner.

The Canadian and Australian companies had grown significantly with the priorities of war production, with both organisations commencing their own designs once hostilities had ceased. A modern elementary trainer was required to replace the venerable Tiger Moths, and the parent company was too busy with other projects to take on the new trainer. There was good reason to allow the Canadian company to be responsible for a trainer not only for the RAF, but also Commonwealth and Allied air forces. A design team headed by Jakimiuk started the project as a good initial exercise to follow the Mosquitos, and the DHC.1 was appropriately named the Chipmunk. It was an all-metal low-wing monoplane with a tandem cockpit for two and powered by a 145-hp Gipsy Major engine.

Hatfield-based Pat Fillingham went to Downsview, Toronto, to make the maiden flight of the first Chipmunk on 22 May 1946, the first of a family of rugged bush planes and local service transports. During flight testing, the Chipmunk proved to have excellent aerobatic qualities and a good rate of climb; it was also robust with simple construction. The RCAF adopted the Chipmunk initially for the flying clubs participating in *ab initio* Air Force and cadet training schemes, and in 1955, they ordered a further batch of Chipmunks for regular RCAF training.

In 1949, twenty-one years after the Canadian company had been started, the RAF adopted the Chipmunk for the RAFVR schools. With good export prospects, in addition to the RAF commitment, there was justification for Chipmunk production to be set up in Britain, particularly for those countries that preferred to pay in British Sterling rather than Canadian dollars. Production was initially at Hatfield, but this transferred to Broughton, where a large Vickers Armstrong shadow factory was acquired by de Havilland in 1948.

By October 1948, Chipmunks had been adopted by seven air forces and civil flying schools in half a dozen countries, but with 130 built in Canada, the dollar shortage restricted demand. By 1955, Chipmunks were in service in some twenty-five countries, and the 1,000th and last British-built Chipmunk came off the line at Broughton in the spring of 1956, this aircraft being the completion of an order for Saudi Arabia. A total of 217 were built in Canada and a further sixty were built under licence in Portugal.

Pat Fillingham flying the Chipmunk prototype CF-DIO-X from Toronto, 16 January 1947. (*DH Photo*)

Canadian Chipmunk prototype CF-DIO-X at the refuelling point on Hatfield aerodrome with a Mosquito night fighter in the background, and construction work on the new concrete runway. (*DH Photo*)

HRH the Duke of Edinburgh learned to fly on the Chipmunk, starting on 12 November 1952 and went solo on 20 December. In later years, he was followed by HRH Prince Charles, who learned to fly in a red-painted Chipmunk. De Havilland Aircraft of Canada went on to design and produce the Beaver, Otter bush aircraft, and tactical transports, followed by the Caribou and Buffalo military transports, the DHC 6 Twin Otter, the DHC 7 four-engined local service airliner, and finally the Dash-8, which in a developed form is still being produced in Canada.

Following 212 Mosquitos during and after the war, de Havilland Australia commenced the design of a light, safe, simple sturdy all-metal transport with an engine out performance in tropical conditions. It was more a Dragon replacement, rather than a Dove competitor and featured three 145-hp Gipsy Majors and a fixed tail-wheel undercarriage. The first flight was on 23 January 1948, but a disappointing overall performance restricted sales, the main operator being the Royal Flying Doctor Service (RFDS). Meanwhile, the Australian company also built Vampires and Goblin engine for the RAAF.

Above: Chipmunk T.10 WP861 D of London UAS visiting Hatfield on 13 July 1968 during the annual Open Day. This aircraft was used by HRH the Duke of Edinburgh for his basic flight training at White Waltham in 1952–53. (*Author's collection*)

HRH Prince Charles learned to fly in Chipmunk WP903 1968/70, which was in the overall red livery of the Queen's Flight and had an enlarged anti-collision beacon on the top of the windscreen. It visited Hatfield on 1 August 1969, and is now flown in its original markings from Henlow. (*Author's collection*)

British Army Beaver Mk 1 XV271, which was part of an order built in Canada but assembled and fitted with British equipment at Broughton. It is flying over Brocket Park near Hatfield on 31 May 1967. (*Author's collection*)

The sole example of Alvis Leonides powered Beaver Mk 2 G-ANAR, which was based at Hatfield, seen 5 August 1971 before return to DH Canada for conversion back to standard Mk 1. (*Author's collection*)

Above: Demonstration of de Havilland Canada Twin Otter F-BTOS of Air Alpes of short take-off from the Hatfield perimeter track to the Chinese with the Trident water test tank in the background. (*Author's collection*)

Below: The de Havilland Drover VQ-FAP of Fiji Airways powered by three Gipsy Major engines. (*DH Photo*)

6

Jet and Rocket Development

With de Havilland piston-engine background experience since the early days of the company, the Gipsy engine family had improved and was giving tremendous reliability. Dove engines achieved an overhaul life of 1,200 hours, Heron 1,600 hours, and Chipmunk Gipsy Major 1,000 hours. By end of 1959, a total of 27,708 Gipsy engines had been built. The two centrifugal compressor jet engines produced during the latter stages of the war were gaining use, including the Goblin in Vampire sales overseas with its modest power output of 3,000-lb thrust. In July and August 1948, the Goblin was given the most severe test to date during a period in the testbeds the equivalent of 462 fighter sorties lasting sixty-five minutes each, using maximum power representing take-off and five minutes simulating combat. The engine was still giving full performance at the end of the test. When the engine was inspected afterwards, it was in such good condition that the test was repeated in March and April 1949, with equally good results. In a 1,000-hour stop-and-start running test, with at least 100 hours at full power, the Goblin engine performed as expected.

With commercial airliner flights being longer in duration and steadier power output demand, the configuration of the engine was considered acceptable for use in a jet airliner. The Ghost engine was similar to the Goblin but with design improvements; thrust was 5,000 lb, making it suitable for the next generation of fighter when it was fitted to the Venom (a development of the Vampire that first flew in September 1949). The Ghost was probably the most advanced centrifugal configuration that could be achieved, even though the thrust was greater than any other turbojet then in production, and it had lower installed drag and weight than any other engine. The way forward was the more efficient, but greater risk, axial flow configuration jet engine. In addition to its military application with bifurcated jet intakes for the Venom family of jet fighters, the Ghost was selected as the first commercial jet engine to power the Comet 1. To adapt the Ghost for the Comet required some 80 per cent redesign, which included a straight-in air intake configuration. A pair of civil Ghost engines were fitted in a converted Lancastrian bomber for endurance testing, and type approval was granted by the Air Registration Board (ARB) on 28 June 1948, the first turbojet in the world to gain civil certification.

The Ghost was not the ideal engine for the Comet, but it was all that was available without long delays to service entry with BOAC. The axial flow Rolls-Royce Avon was a much more efficient and powerful turbojet, but there were delays with its certification. However, with the Ghost-powered Comet 1s entering service to gain experience with the new form of power, the Comet 2 was to follow powered by Avons. The military Ghost continued in production for Venom fighters as did the Goblin for Vampires. When the Comet 1s entered service with BOAC on 2 May 1952, the Ghosts only had an overhaul life of 375 hours, but just over a year later, when BOAC had reached 60,000 engine hours, the overhaul life was increased to 1,000 hours.

With earlier turbojets in regular service, the Halford design team began to look at further developments in jet engines over the following five to fifteen years. A range of engines were also being studied by Rolls-Royce, as well as other manufacturers, but rapid decisions needed to be made on a large engine with supersonic capabilities, which needed to begin development within the first five years from the end of the war. With a rearmament programme underway, the government was not prepared to back such a programme, at least not for some time. Studies were made by the Engine Company engineers at company expense, and a decision was made by Aubrey Burke (by then managing director of the Engine Company) to start detailed design work towards the end of 1950 on an engine with a thrust potential of 25,000 lb, or around 30,000 lb with reheat. Work on the design of the new power plant was not just restricted to design, but also there was a considerable company investment in a new large modern testbed with adequate silencing in a much enlarged Halford Laboratory at Hatfield adjacent to the DH Propellers site; this investment included a new large hangar to house the flight test fleet.

In addition to turbojet developments, there was also a need to look into the capabilities of rocket power that could operate without an air atmosphere. Leadership in rocket design before the war had been in Germany, and one of the DH Engine Company steps taken after the war was to form a study group with the name 'special projects section'. It soon

Military Ghost turbojet Mk 3 for Venom, November 1951. (*DH Photo*)

The world's first commercial turbojet engine, de Havilland Ghost for the Comet with central air intake. (*DH Photo*)

The Manor Road site of BAe Dynamics Group, with the HQ bottom centre. Top centre is the former de Havilland engine hangar, to the left was the propeller flight test hangars; behind the Engine Company hangar is the Halford Laboratory, wind tunnels and propeller test facilities. The BAe 146 water test tank is on the left of the picture. (*BAe Photo*)

became clear that a hydrogen peroxide rocket would be the most practical and safest to use in an aircraft with a catalyst. Solid fuel rockets which once ignited (like fireworks) must burn out without any further control. Liquid propellant rockets with the basic hydrogen peroxide were similar to handle as normal liquid fuels. The first de Havilland rocket motor was called the Sprite and was run on the Hatfield testbeds in November 1949, which was designed as a booster motor for the take-off of heavily laden aircraft. It developed about 55,000 lb per second, which would be similar to 5,000 thrust of a Ghost engine during some eleven seconds of take-off run, and the pilot could turn the rocket off at any time. The Sprite was announced publicly for the first time in November 1949, and provision was made in the Comet 1 to boost hot and high take-offs, with a pair of Sprites located between the two Ghost jet pipes on either side. Tests proved the feasibility of using Sprite-boosted take-offs, but there was concern that passengers may be alarmed by the steam clouds roaring out the back of the aircraft. In the event the Comet never required the take-off aid. However, there was interest for take-off assistance with the RAF V-bombers, which could be boosted by the production version known as the Super Sprite. The developed version was fired up by March 1953 and gave 120,000 lb per second of thrust. It weighed 600 lb, would run for forty seconds, and provide a maximum thrust of 4,000 lb. It was packaged as a jettisonable fairing as a take-off aid for the Vickers Valiant jet bomber, as well as being tested under Victor wings, which flew out of Hatfield.

The perceived threat in the 1950s was from very high-flying bombers carrying nuclear bombs, which were above the operational altitude of the defending missiles and fighters. To destroy hostile bombers flying at between 50,000 and 60,000 feet, the concept of a mixed power plant formula was studied. A typical turbojet engine could be developed to provide a sustained speed of a fighter up to Mach 2, but for endurance and range, it would be used without reheat. To gain altitude rapidly to attack the high-flying bombers would require the boost of a rocket motor, complemented by an axial-flow turbojet like the Gyron or something smaller. Existence of the big turbojet had been kept secret for three years, but the first example ran on the testbed on 3 January 1953, soon proving the validity of the concept. As a result, the Ministry of Supply placed a contract to cover the development of the Gyron, followed by another contract for a smaller engine of similar concept known as the Gyron Junior. The existence of the Gyron was made public in August 1953. The Gyron was a whole new concept in jet engine design, as the enormous ram effect of supersonic flight speeds, reduced the need for a compressor with high-pressure ratio, the engine approaching being a ramjet. The new engine retained much of the simplicity of the Goblin and Ghost with a fully annular combustion chamber, which made the most efficient use of the space between the two-bearing shaft and the outer casing. The investment in this engine—the greatest by the Engine Company— appeared to be justified as it was being considered for a supersonic military strike aircraft project.

The 'special projects department' became the Rocket Division on 1 January 1955 and the Super Sprite achieved type approval testing between 21 September and 14 October 1954. It was issued with the Ministry of Supply Rocket Engine Technical Certificate No. 1 on 12 January 1955. It was thus the first liquid-propelled rocket engine to pass a service type test.

On the morning of 16 April 1955, Frank Halford died, bringing to an end his forty most productive years devoted to the development of aero engines. He had been ill for some three years without letting up, but when he seemed to have regained strength, he unexpectedly passed away in his sleep.

The Spectre rocket was announced in April 1955 as part of the mixed power plant concept with the big Gyron commencing type approval

Lancastrian VM703 taking off on 6 October 1947 with power from six engines, two Merlins, two Ghosts, and two Sprite rockets. (*DH Photo*)

Valiant V-Bomber taking off from Farnborough with the assistance of a pair of underwing Sprite rockets. (*DH Photo*)

John Cunningham taking off from Hatfield in Comet 1 G-ALVG on 7 May 1951, with boost from a pair of Sprite rocket engines. (*DH Photo*)

Saunders Roe SR.53 mixed power-plant experimental fighter prototype XD145 with Spectre 5 variable thrust rocket engine. (*DH Photo*)

testing during the summer in preparation for flight trials to start. Passing its type approval test at a conservative initial thrust rating of 15,000 lb, it was demonstrated at the Farnborough Air Show that September fitted in one of the lower engine nacelles of the Short Sperrin interim jet bomber prototype.

The Gyron Junior made its first testbed run on 12 August, and in less than a year, it passed its qualifying tests for a development contract. This completed a family of advanced engines and a test unit at Hatfield equipped with a high standard of research and test facilities. Both types of new propulsion engines progressed well through 1956; by early 1957, the Gyron was developing 25,000 lb of thrust with reheat, the Gyron Junior had run in the testbed for many hours, and Spectre flight trials were ready to begin. The debate within the British Government regarding when manned military aircraft could be replaced by pilotless missiles held up the decisions regarding future supersonic bombers and fighters, with the only Gyron application being the Hawker P.1121 private venture air superiority strike aircraft with projected Mach 2.5 performance, prototype construction of which was abandoned in 1958.

Then, on 4 April 1957, the infamous Government Defence White Paper declared that Britain's overall defence policy was to concentrate on missile programmes, and most manned aircraft projects would be cancelled. However, this was a premature decision as the aerospace engineers could not predict when missiles would be able to take over the nuclear defence of the country, leaving uncertainty that another generation of manned aircraft would not be developed. There were three projects that concerned the de Havilland Engine programmes which looked likely to be retained, one being the Saunders-Roe SR.177 supersonic all-weather interceptor being developed for the Royal Navy. The SR.177 was to be the first mixed-power plant fighter, with an 8,000-lb thrust controllable Spectre rocket engine to rapidly get the fighter to the radar-detected altitude of advancing hostile nuclear bombers, and the 14,000-lb thrust Gyron Junior for cruising at altitude to attack the bombers. The aircraft was virtually a pilot-guided weapon system and was a practical step towards a pilotless ground-to-air missile, the human monitor later to be replaced by a computer.

The programme fulfilled twelve years of work by de Havilland Engines, as well as several years of effort by the partly owned Saunders-Roe, being a major step in technological progress. All the features—including airframe, power plants, radar and wingtip-mounted de Havilland Firestreak air-to-air missiles—were all available, and there were prospects of export interest, particularly the West German Government.

However, in 1958, the British Government decided that even though it was a fine project, it would not be ordered into production, but a pair of

First testbed run of the Gyron engine, 5 January 1953. *Rear*: Halford, Brodie, Burke, Moult, Owner, Miller, and Arscott. *Front*: Bristow, Cockburn, and Morton. (*DH Photo*)

Short Sperrin interim jet bomber prototype VX158 Gyron testbed with the test engines in the lower nacelles below the Avons. (*DH Photo*)

Spectre Canberra VN813 flying testbed, December 1956. (*DH Photo*)

SR.53 scaled-down research aircraft were allowed to go ahead, the first one making its maiden flight from Boscombe Down on 16 May 1957. Power for the SR.53 (a conventional delta wing monoplane) was from a Spectre rocket engine and a Viper turbojet for cruise. Thus, de Havilland lost prospective orders not only for the engines, but also their shares in Saunders-Roe. When it was realised that missile defences could reach the high-altitude bombers, identified well in advance by radars, the strategy was to come down to a very low level to make approaches undetected until the last minute, negating the need for high-altitude mixed power-plant defending fighters.

A second project was for two de Havilland Gyron Juniors to power the Blackburn NA 39 low-level strike aircraft, to become the Royal Navy's Buccaneer, the first example flying on 30 April 1958. The engines were designed to allow air bleed for flap-blowing and other aerodynamic assistance during take-off and landing on aircraft carriers. An initial batch of Gyron Junior-powered Buccaneer S.1s were produced, but the engine did not have sufficient power, and the Buccaneer S.2 was developed powered by two Rolls-Royce Spey turbojets to serve the FAA and later the RAF.

The third project concerning de Havilland Engines was power for the Bristol 188 high-speed research aircraft, which was constructed from puddle welded stainless steel, and was powered by a pair of Gyron Juniors. The use of stainless steel was to overcome the problems with high aerodynamic skin temperatures, but production difficulties experienced during the construction of the two airframes delayed the project, and problems with the reheat of the engines resulted in the Bristol aircraft barely achieving Mach 1. Both 188s flew but did not achieve their performance goals, one surviving at the RAF Museum at Cosford.

The final Engine Company project was a small propeller turbine for helicopter power. An agreement with General Electric of America resulted in licensed production and development of the 1,000-hp T.58 turbine in Britain. The British development was known as the Gnome, developed at Stag Lane and Hatfield with an additional gearbox and driveshaft. The first de Havilland-developed Gnome made its initial run at the Hatfield Halford Laboratory on 5 June 1959 and was selected to power the licence-built Westland Sikorsky S-55 helicopter known in British service as the Whirlwind. A later development was the larger Westland S-58 Wessex, powered by two Gnome engines.

In the government-ordered mergers of Britain's Aerospace Industry in the late 1950s, the de Havilland Engine Company was merged into Bristol Siddeley Engines, based at Filton, although work continued at Leavesden on the Gem, to become the power plant for the Westland Lynx helicopter, both in Britain and overseas. In turn, Bristol Siddeley Engines became part of Rolls-Royce when the British aircraft industry was nationalised.

7

Jet Fighter Developments

Having subcontracted Vampire production to English Electric at Preston, the de Havilland board began to look for further production capacity within the company. It was impractical to extend the Hatfield factory, so it was decided to lease a large factory elsewhere; the government shadow factory at Broughton near Chester was available with the adjacent RAF Hawarden airfield housing 48 MU. It was the most modern factory available in Europe at the time with 1 million sq. feet being ideal for the company's plans. There was ample headroom, whereas Hatfield had been built piecemeal latterly for Mosquito production. Broughton also featured overhead cranes on roof-mounted tracks allowing movement of whole airframes around the production areas. It was traditional that during the day shift, the overhead cranes were operated by ladies, as they were more accurate in their positioning. By 1 July 1948, de Havilland had taken possession of the factory and began to move in Mosquito and Hornet production jigs, the first Broughton Mosquito, an NF 38 flying on 30 September. In the first year, a modest eighty-five aircraft were delivered, but in 1950, with British rearmament underway, 367 aircraft were completed, then 683 aircraft in 1951. Comet 2s, 4s, and Nimrod prototypes were built at Broughton, together with all the DH 125 business jets. The site has now become the main production facility for Airbus wings with a massive investment in composite manufacture.

With developments by the de Havilland Engine making improved turbojet engines, the Aircraft Company design team were able to study improvements to the Vampire and the later Venom. A simple derivation to the Vampire fighter was for the FAA following successful deck trials, which was a small number of Sea Vampire F.20s for interim use of jet-powered aircraft, although they were not flown regularly on deck operations.

Hawarden airfield with 48 MU in the foreground and the Broughton factory on the other side of the runway. This site has now changed radically with new facilities for the production of Airbus wings. (*DH Photo*)

A typical day's work for the test pilots at Hawarden on 15 March 1951. The line ups include export Vampires, Chipmunks for the RAF and export, plus Hornets and Sea Hornet. In addition, there could be Doves, Herons, and Venoms, plus Beverleys and Shackletons coming off overhaul. (*DH Photo*)

The vast production factory at Broughton, which was built in the Second World War for Vickers Armstrong to produce Wellington bombers. Comet 2 XK716, which was delivered to 216 Squadron on 7 May 1957, has the re-skinning of the cabin almost complete, with other Comet 2s, Venoms, and Sea Venoms also being assembled. (*DH Photo*)

Ex-Air France Comet 1A F-BGNZ after the cabin was re-skinned and re-registered G-APAS. It later became XM823 with de Havilland Propellers for infra-red seeker head research and made its last flight to Shawbury on 8 April 1968 for preservation at the RAF Museum at Cosford, the last complete Comet 1 to survive. (*HSA Photo*)

A series of other Vampire developments began within months of the end of the war, the Vampire fuselage being made wider to accommodate two crew as a two-seat side-by-side night fighter DH 113 developed as a private venture, the first flight being by Geoffrey Pike on 28 August 1949. Power came from a 3,350-lb thrust Goblin 3 turbojet with the pilot and radar operator accommodated snugly side-by-side in a wooden nacelle and an extended nose housing an AI Mk 10 radar under a radome. The standard armament of four under-fuselage 20-mm cannons was retained, and it was first demonstrated to the public at the Farnborough Air Show in September, only a few days after the first flight. Provision was made for a pair of 100-gallon underwing long-range fuel tanks. The cockpit canopy was a Mosquito frame type with entry through a top hatch.

The Vampire night fighter was intended for export and an order was received for twelve aircraft from the Egyptian Air Force in October 1949, but when the British Government banned the export of arms to Egypt, they were taken over by the RAF as Vampire NF 10s as an interim type pending the delivery of Meteor and Venom night fighters. They entered service with 25 Squadron at West Malling in July 1951 to replace Mosquito NF 36s, followed by 23 Squadron at Coltishall and 151 Squadron at Leuchars. A total of twenty-five Vampire NF 10s were built at Hatfield before the transfer of production to Broughton where a further sixty-two were built, with some going to Italy. The Vampire NF 10 only served with the RAF for about two and a half years before some surplus aircraft were used for navigation training, and others were refurbished as interim night fighters for the Indian Air Force.

The removal of the AI radar and fitting of dual controls was a logical step in providing an advanced jet trainer as a private venture. A slightly modified wooden fuselage pod was used, and the first DH 115 Vampire Trainer was designed and built at the old Airspeed factory at Christchurch in Hampshire. It was revealed publicly statically for the first time at the Farnborough Air Show in September 1970 and was first flown from Christchurch by John Wilson on 15 November the same year.

The original canopy was similar to the Vampire NF 10 but was later replaced by a clear view canopy over newly installed twin ejection seats. On satisfactory completion of company trials, prototype WW456 was handed over to 204 AFS, then for service trials on 26 April 1951; and the type was adopted by the RAF in February 1952 as the standard advanced trainer designated the Vampire T.11. This was the first time that RAF pilots qualified for wings on a jet aircraft, following their initial training on Percival Provosts.

The cockpit was pressurised and a pair of 100-gallon fuel tanks could be carried externally under the wings. The aircraft could be used for fighter navigation, the demonstration of compressibility effects, and for combat training when fitted with dual gunsights and two 20-mm cannons.

Line-up of Vampires and Venoms outside the Hatfield factory with a Comet 1 tail protruding through the side doors of the erecting shop. The aircraft are Vampire F.3, Sea Vampire F.20, Vampire NF 10, Vampire T.11, Venom FB 1, Venom NF 2, and Sea Venom FAW.20. (*DH Photo*)

Vampire NF 10 private venture prototype G-5-2 was first flown by Geoffrey Pike from Hatfield on 28 August 1949. (*DH Photo*)

For other armament training, provision was made for the carriage of eight 20-lb RP and eight 25-lb practice bombs, or 2,500-lb bombs with RP, or two 1,000-lb bombs, making it a useful export ground attack aircraft. Deliveries began to the RAF in early 1952, equipping advanced flying schools, Fighter Weapons School at Leconfield, 5 FTS at Oakington in 1954, and RAF College at Cranwell. Vampire Trainers were also issued to RAF fighter squadrons for communications and instrument ratings. The FAA also adopted Vampire Trainers following evaluation at Culham in 1952, ordering seventy-three T Mk 22s. When production was completed in 1958, 804 Vampire Trainers had been built at Christchurch, with 427 at Broughton, the first of which had flown in October 1951. The total included large numbers of export T.55s, which equipped the air forces of more than twenty countries. The Vampire T.11s were finally retired from RAF training duties with 3 FTS at Leeming on 29 November 1967.

John Cunningham took experimental Ghost-engined Vampire TG278 to the record height of 59,446 feet on 23 March 1948; he was flying the aircraft in a programme to investigate improved speed, ceiling, and rate of climb at high altitude without losing the docility nearer the ground, which was a feature of the original Vampires. This aircraft not only allowed the development of the later Venom but was helpful in determining the performance and reliability of the Ghost engines for the planned Comet jet airliner.

Another experimental aircraft created from a basic Vampire fuselage nacelle was the DH 108, unofficially known as the 'Swallow' due to its outline in the air. The initial concept of the DH 108 tailless aircraft was to fit metal swept wings to the fuselage to investigate the layout for the proposed jet airliner. The swept wings were also used to check the aerodynamics for a projected fighter design. Design work on the DH 108 began in October 1945 to fulfil Spec. E.18/45, the sweepback of the wing being 43 degrees with an overall area 15 per cent greater than the Vampire. A fixed fin was fitted above the jet pipe with conventional rudder, and elevons combining the duties of elevators and ailerons, fitted on the wing trailing-edge outboard of flaps.

After completion at Hatfield, the first prototype TG283 was taken by road to the remote long runway at Woodbridge where Geoffrey de Havilland Jnr took it up for the first time on 15 May 1946. This low-speed prototype featured fixed Handley Page slats on the wing-leading edge and anti-spin chutes on each wingtip to guard against Dutch roll or loss of control with a wing drop at low speeds. In practice, it was able to formate alongside a Proctor for air-to-air photos and on return to Hatfield took part in dog fights with a Mosquito. Following company flight trials, the characteristics of the swept wing TG 283 was transferred to the RAE at Farnborough in October 1948 where stability, control, and landing trials were carried out, which led to the fitting of a long-stroke Sea Vampire main undercarriage. The aircraft was

A pair of Vampire T.55s destined for the Syrian Air Force outside the Experimental Department on 8 April 1960, which were embargoed by the British Government and later scrapped. (*DH Photo*)

John Cunningham flew Ghost testbed Vampire TG/278 to a record height of 59,446 feet on 23 March 1948. (*DH Photo*)

The first DH 108 TG283 returns to Hatfield on 19 May 1946 after making first flight from Woodbridge by Geoffrey de Havilland Jnr on 15 May 1946 and was used for low-speed research into the characteristics of the swept-back wing. (*DH Photo*)

DH 108 being flown by Geoffrey de Havilland Jnr. (*DH Photo*)

lost with its pilot (Sqn Ldr G. E. C. Genders) on 1 May 1950, when during stall trials it crashed at Hartley Wintney. There was no ejection seat fitted.

The second prototype TG306 was built to the same specification but configured for high-speed research with a potential for supersonic speed. This aircraft, once again based on a Vampire fuselage from the English Electric production line, featured power controls of the type planned for the Comet, and the wing sweepback increased to 45 degrees. Power came from a 3,300-lb thrust Goblin 3 and was flown for the first time from Hatfield by Geoffrey de Havilland Jnr on 23 August 1946. It was soon flying speeds in excess of 616 mph, the world's absolute speed record at the time. Following the first public appearance at the SBAC Display at Radlett, the aircraft was prepared for an attempt to gain a new speed record over the official course along the south coast near Tangmere. Geoffrey de Havilland Jnr took off from Hatfield on 27 September with the intention of making practice flights at low level over the Thames Estuary after diving from 10,000 feet. Twenty minutes later, the aircraft was seen to break up by witnesses, the wreckage falling into Egypt Bay near Gravesend in Kent, killing Geoffrey instantly.

Most of the wreckage was recovered, including the engine that had been operating normally. The subsequent enquiry established that there had been a structural failure of the wings from the fuselage under high speeds experienced in the region of Mach 0.9. The aircraft had experienced gusts, with Geoffrey hitting his head on the inside of the canopy and breaking his neck; the nose pitched forward and the wings

The wreckage of DH 108 TG206 in Egypt Bay after crash 27 September 1946, killing Geoffrey de Havilland Jnr. (*DH Photo*)

fell downwards. John Cunningham, who was chief test pilot of the de Havilland Engine Company, was appointed chief test pilot of the Aircraft Company, becoming responsible for managing the test flying for all de Havilland companies.

Trials with TG306 had shown that performance would be much improved by lowering the pilot's seat, redesigning the canopy, and lengthening the nose to make it more pointed, resulting in the third prototype (VW120), powered by a 3,750-lb thrust Goblin 4, which was first flown by John Cunningham on 24 July 1947. One of his early tasks was to try to reproduce the conditions that caused the accident to TG306 to fully establish the causes. As testing progressed, the aircraft was entered for the 100-km International Closed Circuit speed record flying from Hatfield of 12 April 1948 flown by John Derry, who had joined de Havilland from Supermarine Aircraft, achieving a new record speed of 605.23 mph. The same pilot went on to exceed the speed of sound for the first time outside the USA on 9 September 1948. He flew to 40,000 feet, having taken off from Hatfield, and entered a dive, breaking the 'sound barrier' at 30,000 feet and completely losing control. With the denser air at lower altitudes resulting in a lower Mach number, he regained control and landed back at Hatfield. Major Chuck Yeager had exceeded the speed of sound in the USA, flying the rocket-powered Bell X-1, which had been taken aloft under an adapted B-29 bomber, and when the rocket fuel ran out, he glided back to Edwards Air Force Base. The DH 108 had taken off and landed at Hatfield under its own power and exceeded the speed of sound on the power of a 3,750-lb thrust Goblin engine. In the late summer of 1949, VW120 was handed over the RAE Farnborough where it joined the original low-speed prototype, but it was lost on 15 February 1950 in a crash near Birkhill, Bucks, killing Sqn Ldr J. S. R Muller-Roland due to a failure of the pilot's oxygen supply. The tailless layout was found to be unsuitable for an airliner concept.

The logical interim development of the Vampire family of jet fighters was the Venom, pending the development of the second-generation jet fighter Hunter, Swift, and Javelin, all of which were delayed into RAF service. Although produced to a similar layout as the Vampire, the Venom was a completely new design to take advantage of the more powerful de Havilland Ghost turbojet. The fuselage nacelle was still made from wood, but had thinner wings swept back 17 degrees on the leading edge, and 75-gallon wing fuel tanks could be fitted on the wingtips but were not jettisonable in flight. The first prototype Venom FB Mk 1 (VV612) built to Spec. F.15/49 was flown from Hatfield on 2 September 1949 by John Derry and following flight development and service trials at Boscombe Down was ordered in quantity production for the RAF as a replacement

The third DH 108 VX120 first flown by John Cunningham on 24 July 1947 and used for high speed research into swept-back wing aerodynamics. This aircraft exceeded the speed of sound on 9 September 1948 when flown by John Derry. (*Charles E. Brown Photo*)

for Vampire FB.5s. Power came from a 4,850-lb thrust Ghost 103 engine and armament was four undernose-mounted fixed 20-mm Hispano Mk V cannons; two 1,000-lb bombs or eight 60-lb RP could be carried under the wings. Main production was at Broughton, with additional aircraft being assembled by Fairey Aviation at Ringway. Most Venom fighter bombers were issued to the 2nd TAF in Germany for ground attack duties, followed by the Middle East Air Force (MEAF) in 1954. In 1955, the improved Venom FB 4 was produced powered by a 4,950-lb thrust Ghost 104, the first one flying on 29 December 1953. This version could carry jettisonable underwing fuel tanks as well as the ones on the wingtips and the fin and rudder shape was modified to prevent excessive yaw and rudder locking at slow speeds. Later production FB.4s were also fitted with ejection seats, with FB.4s replacing FB.1s in Germany from 1954.

Although the Venom was produced as a relatively short life interim aircraft, it was successful with exports. Two were delivered to Italy; the Royal Iraqi Air Force took deliveries between 8 April 1955 and 3 February 1956; the Venezuelan Air Force ordered twenty-two FB.54s—the export version of the FB.4; and the major overseas user was the Swiss Air Force who licence-built 126 FB.1s starting in 1953, later followed by twenty-

The first prototype Venom FB 1 (VV612), which was flown from Hatfield for the first time on 2 September 1949. (*DH Photo*)

four reconnaissance versions in 1956. A final batch of 100 Venom FB.4s were built in Switzerland from 1965, the last aircraft being withdrawn from service towards the end of 1983.

A private venture development was the two-seat Venom NF 2 to replace the Vampire night fighters in RAF service. The prototype Venom NF 2 (G-5-3) was first flown by John Derry on 22 August 1950, who demonstrated it at Farnborough the following month. Standard Venom wings and tail booms were fitted to a wider two-seat side-by-side fuselage with AI radar in the nose, retaining the four under-fuselage 20-mm cannon armament. Following flight trials, Venom NF 2s entered service with 23 Squadron at Coltishall in 1953. The improved Venom NF 3 featured some of the improvements of the FB 4; in addition, it had power-operated ailerons, a clear-view jettisonable rear-hinged canopy, and improved AI radar. The first one flew on 22 February 1953, with the initial production versions entering service with 141 Squadron in 1955.

Developed from the Venom Night Fighter was the Sea Venom FAW Mk 20, which was designed at Christchurch to Spec. N.107 for the FAA to bridge the gap between the Sea Hornet and later Sea Vixen. The airframe was strengthened for catapult take-off from the deck of an aircraft carrier, folding wings were featured, and an arrester hook was fitted in a fairing over the jet pipe. Power was from a 4,840-lb Ghost and three prototypes were ordered, the first two being built at Hatfield and the third at Christchurch.

DH Venom NF 2 prototype WP227, which was first flown from Hatfield on 22 August 1950 and was delivered to A&AEE Boscombe Down on 3 April 1951. It was later evaluated by the Fleet Air Arm, resulting in the adoption as the Sea Venom. (*MOS Photo*)

WK376 first flew from Hatfield on 19 April 1952 and was delivered to Boscombe Down a month later, from where it undertook carrier trials on HMS *Illustrious* on 9 July. The third aircraft was the first to be fitted with folding wings, making its first flight on 26 July 1952. Production started at Christchurch, later moving to Broughton. A total of fifty Sea Venom FAW.20s were produced, entering service with 890 NAS at Yeovilton on 20 March 1954. Due to some shortcomings with the earlier versions, the improved Sea Venom FAW.21 (the naval equivalent of the NF 3) was produced, including the installation of ejection seats for the two crew members. Power was increased by fitting a 4,950-lb thrust Ghost 104, which was later replaced by the 5,300-lb thrust Ghost 105 in the FAW.22. A total of 167 FAW.21s were built for the FAA—sixty-eight at Christchurch and ninety-nine at Broughton. Thirty-nine FAW.22s were built at Broughton; the last was delivered to RNAS Stretton on 7 January 1958. Sea Venoms were used during the Suez Crisis in October 1956, and the last were withdrawn from front-line FAA service with the decommissioning of 891 NAS on 28 July 1961.

A significant export order for the Sea Venom was for thirty-nine FAW.53s for the Royal Australian Navy (RAN) placed on 27 February 1956, which was the export version of the FAW.21. The first was delivered to Boscombe Down on 1 March 1955 with all the aircraft built at Christchurch; the final aircraft was delivered on 18 January 1956. All served on HMAS *Melbourne* and final retirement was on 25 August 1967. The French Government adopted the Sea Venom and modified it into the Aquilon, which was licence-built by Sud Aviation at Marignane near Marseilles, continuing in service until 1963.

The second partially navalised prototype Sea Venom (WK379) at Hatfield in July 1952. (*DH Photo*)

The fully navalised third prototype Sea Venom (WK385) complete with folding wings at Hatfield on 8 October 1952. (*DH Photo*)

Sea Venom visiting Hatfield on 20 March 1967 from 750 NAS at Lossiemouth with the Blue Streak tower in the background. (*Author's collection*)

Sea Venoms being modified in the factory at Broughton, 7 December 1956. (*DH Photo*)

8

Comet:
The World's First Jet Airliner

The de Havilland companies produced many fine products, but probably the four most significant aircraft were the First World War DH 4 bomber, which was faster than many of the fighters; the Moth, which revolutionised private flying; the Mosquito—a legend; and the Comet Jet Airliner, which pioneered commercial flying today.

When the Vampire and the Goblin engine were being designed by the combined efforts of the Aircraft and Engine companies in 1941 and 1942, thoughts were also given to civil applications, with close working together on estimates of performance, structural weight, fuel weight, and a useful payload. The initial jet engine fuel consumption appeared too high for practical air transport except for very short uneconomical stages. As early as May to June 1941, Clarkson, Newman, and the team studied the feasibility of fitting two Goblin jets to a modified Flamingo (the high-wing, all-metal aircraft produced just before the war). Except on the shortest stages, all the disposable load would be taken up by fuel, making a faster high-flying aircraft necessary, the 'jet' Flamingo being a yardstick. With wartime production a priority, there was no time to undertake any practical work on a jet transport, with the thoughts remaining academic.

However, at the end of 1942, the government perceived the need to consider a post-war transport aircraft programme. A committee chaired by Lord Brabazon was set up to define the categories of civil aircraft that Britain should produce without being in direct competition with the more advanced, at the time, American industry. Potential airlines, including BOAC, were encouraged to formulate plans and requirements, which could pave the way for long term projects, including a jet airliner. On 11 March 1943, a statement was made in the House of Lords, stating the government planned to direct some design effort to transport aircraft. The Brabazon Committee reported in May 1943 a recommendation in general terms for a jet-powered transatlantic mail plane cruising at over 400 mph, carrying 1 ton of payload under the designation Type 4. The Hatfield design department was also considering a light twin-engined category, designated Type 5b, which became the Dove and a possible twin Bristol Hercules piston engine development of the Flamingo with a lengthened fuselage, intended to be a DC-3 replacement. From August 1943, de Havilland was relieved of this project, which was replaced by the Brabazon Type 2, later to become the Ambassador, produced by Airspeed, a company by then owned by de Havilland.

The Brabazon Committee was increased in size from 2 June 1943 to include representatives of manufacturers and airlines. Captain de Havilland was then able to present the results of the tentative calculations for a jet transport by the Hatfield design team. It was emphasised that there would have to be wind tunnel investigations into various layouts of thin-wing airframes, although there was still concern that only short-range operations could be managed due to high fuel consumption of the early jet engines. In the second half of 1943, a detailed design was considered with a twenty-seat aircraft of a similar layout to the Vampire, powered by three Goblins clustered in the rear of the nacelle, giving a range of around 700 miles. Three of the new, as yet to run, Ghost engines were then considered. This formula was discussed on 19 April 1944 and agreement given to proceed with the jet airliner, although it was not then practical to specify a detailed list of requirements. The Hatfield team still felt that long-range operations was the target to achieve, particularly as the jet engine gave a vibration-free smooth ride, reducing fatigue for passengers. The key was for runways to be extended to allow jet airliners to operate, and BOAC were very enthusiastic about the prospect of jet transatlantic operations of a 500-mph mail-plane at costs that would make the service economical.

By August 1944, the Ghost-powered 'Vampire' mail carrier was favoured, and by October, it was defined to have accommodation for six passengers and 2,000 lb of mail, with a high-speed wind tunnel model despatched to Farnborough for testing on 28 February 1945. Studies also progressed on a more conventional layout powered by four Ghosts with an alternative fuselage of 8.5 feet diameter to carry twenty-four passengers, or a 10-foot diameter fuselage with room for twenty-four to thirty-six passengers seated four abreast. This would give Britain a competitive lead in global airline markets over existing American designs. The practical problems of flying high and fast did not appear to be insuperable, although they were challenging. As the aircraft would be flying in smooth air at high altitude, the cabin would have to be pressurised for comfort with air quality controlled for temperature and humidity, navigation and control systems would need to cope with higher speeds and low-speed handling would be essential without the braking effect of propeller discs. A swept-back wing was being considered to delay the effects of compressibility at higher speeds.

Following an intensive investigation, based on the knowledge available, a progress report was presented to the Committee on 1 October 1945, based on a swept back 40-degree wing tailless airliner with an all-up weight of 75,000 lb powered by four Ghosts mounted beneath the wings near the trailing edge. To investigate this layout, the DH 108 experimental jet based on a Vampire nacelle was proposed as already detailed. The plan of eliminating all horizontal surfaces had to be abandoned in March 1946 as the tailless layout limited the effectiveness of the flaps, resulting in a given wing area and runway length. The take-off and landing weights had to be less than if a tailplane with normal elevators was used, rendering the concept uneconomical.

The first complete brochure featured a 40-degree swept-back wing with horizontal tail surfaces, giving a transatlantic payload of 5,000 lb with an all-up weight of 93,000 lb. However, after the DH 108 had been flying for about ten weeks, the sweepback proved uneconomical, partly because of the required greater wing structural weight. By eliminating the sweepback, the transatlantic payload increased from 5,000 to 9,000 lb. In the summer of 1946, a more orthodox layout was therefore decided upon with a reduced swept-back wing of 20 degrees to help with both centre of gravity and aerodynamics, making it easier to predict performance and delivery targets at the project stage.

Approval was achieved from BOAC and the government during August and September 1946, and on Friday 27 September, with C. C. Walker in his office, Sir Geoffrey de Havilland reached agreement on a final major point, allowing detail design to proceed. That evening, his older son Geoffrey was killed flying the high-speed DH 108 while practising for the world absolute speed record.

Design work continued on the jet airliner, and by November, a complete weight and performance statement for what was to become the DH 106 was prepared. With an all-up weight of 100,000 lb, the payload was estimated to be 7,000 lb, which was equivalent to twenty-four passengers, carried from London to Gander in Canada against a 100-mph headwind, allowing for diversions. For the empire routes, the all-up weight was planned at 96,500 lb, giving stage lengths of 2,200 miles with a payload of 10,000 lb, equivalent to thirty-two passengers. Guarantees of payload, range, cruising speed, and take-off performance had to be defined, all of which were met by the time the aircraft entered service.

Detailed design commenced during the month of Geoffrey's death, the aircraft flying two and three-quarter years later, with service entry a further two and three-quarter years after that, making a very creditable five and a half years development in total. The DH 106 Comet, as it had become was a challenging new design, did not represent a larger step forward than experienced at the time. It was not necessary to build a prototype first, which would have delayed the programme, while the new aircraft proved itself, the first aircraft being basically the first production example; however, on the basis of orders for sixteen aircraft, it was not economical to tool up for high numbers of aircraft. Initial orders were placed in 1946 and 1947 by BOAC for eight Comet 1s and another six for British South American Airways, the latter merging with BOAC, allowing a contract for fourteen Comets to be finalised. The Ministry of Supply ordered the first two development aircraft at a commercial price like the others. It was anticipated that some fifty Comets would have to be sold to reach break even on the investment in tooling.

The first Comet was hand-built in the experimental department at Hatfield in great secrecy, and it was finally pushed out backwards on to the apron on 2 April 1949 to be prepared for engine runs. The *de Havilland Gazette* for April carried an introductory statement on the Comet, giving its size, purpose, and expected flying qualities, with a low-wing loading allowing use of existing airport runways along the world's routes.

During design and development, de Havilland undertook a comprehensive structural test programme based on knowledge at the time but taking into account the dynamic stresses associated with cabin pressurisation. Initially, details were tested, followed by assemblies, with the first production wing being fixed to a fuselage section, and the wing flexed up and down by 3 feet at the tips by powerful hydraulic rams many thousands of times. A decompression chamber was installed at Hatfield for testing systems in cold high-altitude conditions, as low as -70 degrees C and as high as 70,000 feet. The first section tested in this chamber was the flight deck nose section tested to 9-lb pressure for 2,000 applications, as well as fuselage sections.

Testing of large cabin sections was done underwater, the section being filled with pressurised water, any failure being contained locally. Both the nose and fuselage sections were tested in water tanks up to 16.5 lb per square inch, double the pressure experienced in service. Windows and frames were tested in a number of ways, including pressurising them every working day for three years, with one window tested to 100 lb per square inch. All the structural testing was founded on the belief that static testing with a large margin for safety would be more than adequate to allow for any fatigue stresses which might be present on the structures.

In preparation for the flight-testing stage, John Cunningham gained experience of modern airline operations, studying crew and technical

Comet prototype being assembled in the Experimental Department, 11 March 1949. To pull the aircraft out, the fin was lowered from the roof structure and attached to a slot in the concrete floor to guide it out. (*DH Photo*)

Comet nose wheel-steering ground test rig with Mosquito undercarriage outriggers, 2 February 1948. (*DH Photo*)

Horsa II glider TL348 fitted with a mock-up Comet nose to check for vision and rain clearance, flown by John Cunningham and towed aloft by a Halifax bomber. (*DH Photo*)

Comet 1 prototype on engine runs in preparation for first flight. (*DH Photo*)

Early Comet 1 production at Hatfield with wings in the foreground, 14 March 1950. (*DH Photo*)

Comet fuselage assembly on floor tracks in the old flying school building. (*DH Photo*)

management on flights as a supernumerary crew member with five transatlantic flights and two round trips to Australia. On 27 July 1949, John's thirtieth birthday, the media was invited to Hatfield to witness taxiing and hops of the first Comet. After they had gone home, John was informed unexpectedly the aircraft was ready and cleared for flight, so he elected to take off without any 'audience'; the London press took a long time to forgive de Havilland.

John was joined by John Wilson, a new test pilot to join the Hatfield team; Frank Reynolds, flight engineer; Harry Waters, electrical flight engineer and Tony Fairbrother, flight test observer. The aircraft was flown to 10,000 feet and handling checked over low and medium speeds, followed by a 100 feet flypast along the Hatfield runway and landed after thirty-one minutes to a welcome by a few hundred employees. On meeting with Sir Geoffrey de Havilland the next day, John found they shared a birthday. During the following eighteen working days, the aircraft flew 32.5 hours, in the first eleven months 324 hours, equivalent to about an hour a day, seven days a week.

Throughout the flight development programme, the aircraft remained serviceable and never required any major modifications. By the end of 1949, the take-off weight had been increased to 105,000 lb carrying thirty-six passengers over stage lengths of 1,500 miles cruising at just below 500 mph. Although the cost of fuel per flying hour was around double for a comparable piston-engined airliner, speed made up for this, resulting in the cost per passenger mile being competitive. The Comet introduced a new era of speed and smoothness in air travel, with unprecedented mechanical simplicity and the elimination of highly inflammable fuel all at a competitive cost.

During the flight development programme, three months after the first flight, the Comet flew from London Airport to Tripoli and back on 25 October within half a day, followed by many more record-breaking flights to other distant destinations. Flight trials went so well that they were able to commence proving flights from Heathrow on 2 April 1951, and on 7 May 1951, the Comet prototype took off from Hatfield boosted by a pair of 5,000-lb thrust Sprite rocket motors, proving a concept that was never used practically. With a certificate of airworthiness awarded on 22 January 1952, BOAC were able to commence regular services from Heathrow on 2 May 1952 to Johannesburg in Comet 1 G-ALYP via Rome, Beirut, Khartoum, Entebbe, and Livingstone in an elapsed time of 23.5 hours.

The first overseas order was for two increased all-up weight Comet 1As for Canadian Pacific (CPA), the first being rolled into the under-construction flight test hangar in December 1952, although one was lost on its delivery flight, and the other allocated to BOAC. The flight test hangar was the largest all-aluminium structure when it was built and

Comet 1 prototype G-5-1 was flown for the first time by John Cunningham from Hatfield on Sunday evening, 27 July 1949. (*DH Photo*)

Comet 1 prototype G-ALVG fitted with a four-wheel bogie production configuration undercarriage, although the undercarriage could not be retracted in flight due to insufficient clearance in the wings. (*DH Photo*)

M.C.A. Form No. 958

UNITED KINGDOM

MINISTRY OF CIVIL AVIATION

CERTIFICATE OF AIRWORTHINESS

No. A.3215

NATIONALITY AND REGISTRATION MARKS	CONSTRUCTOR AND CONSTRUCTOR'S DESIGNATION OF AIRCRAFT	AIRCRAFT SERIAL No. (CONSTRUCTOR'S No.)
G-ALYS	The de Havilland Aircraft Co. Ltd. Comet D.H.106 Series 1.	06005

CATEGORY : Normal

SUBDIVISION :
(a) Public transport for passengers
(b) Public transport for mails
(c) Public transport for goods
(d) Private (e) Aerial work
(h) Demonstration (i) Crew familiarisation

This Certificate of Airworthiness is issued pursuant to the Convention on International Civil Aviation dated 7th December, 1944, and the Air Navigation Order, 1949, the Air Navigation (General) Regulations, 1949, and the Air Navigation (Radio) Regulations, 1949, in respect of the above-mentioned aircraft, which is considered to be airworthy when maintained and operated in accordance with the requirements of the above-mentioned Order and Regulations, and the pertinent Flight Manual.

John S Maclay.

~~Parliamentary~~ Minister of Civil Aviation.

Date 22nd January, 1952.

This certificate is valid for the period(s) shewn below		Signature, Official Stamp and Date
From 22nd January, 1952	to 21st January, 1953.	
From	to	
From	to	
From	to	
From	to	

No entries or endorsements may be made on this Certificate except in the manner and by the persons authorised for the purpose by the Minister of Civil Aviation.

If this Certificate is lost, the Secretary, Ministry of Civil Aviation (R.L.2) should be informed at once, the Certificate Number being quoted.

Any person finding this Certificate should forward it immediately to the Secretary, Ministry of Civil Aviation, (R.L.2), Ariel House, Strand, London, W.C.2.

(9158) Wt. 9796 3/938-900 4 49 C.& Co. 745(8).

The world's first Certificate of Airworthiness for a jet airliner: G-ALYS, 22 January 1952. (*DH Photo*)

BOAC Comet 1 G-ALYP departs London Heathrow on 2 May 1952 on the world's first jet commercial service to Johannesburg. (*BOAC Photo*)

First production Comet 1 (G-ALYP) at Hatfield 19 April 1952, which was first flown on 9 January 1951 and took part in the flight development programme. (*DH Photo*)

BOAC Comet 1s in the flight test fleet at Hatfield in August 1951 with de Havilland Propeller test fleet in the background, including a Halifax and Hastings prototype. (*DH Photo*)

capable of accommodation six Comets plus other aircraft. It was unique in that it was the only integrated flight test facility in the world that included not only a large hangar, but also featured air traffic control, fire station, instrument laboratory, workshops, and accommodation for test pilots and flight development engineers. This building was Grade II* listed on the closure of the aerodrome and is now a fitness centre with the structure preserved. Other Comet 1As were sold to UAT in France with three aircraft, two to the RCAF, and another three to Air France, completing the Comet 1 production run.

On 16 February 1952, modified Comet 1 G-ALYT was flown from Hatfield by John Cunningham powered by four 6,500-lb thrust Rolls-Royce Avon turbojets as the prototype of the Comet 2, making the first major development. The production version of the Comet 2 had an all-up weight of 120,000 lb with each Avon developing 7,300-lb thrust, increasing the still air range to 2,535 miles and the 3-foot longer fuselage could carry a payload of 13,500 lb. The first of twelve Comet 2s for BOAC made its first flight from Hatfield on 27 August 1953 and was allocated to the development programme including tropical trials. Further sales were received from CPA for three Comet 2s as well as six Comet 2s for Air France, the Comet showing every sign of becoming a world-beater, gaining universal acceptance with the airlines and passengers, achieving consistently high load factors.

CPA Comet 1A CF-CUN at the entrance of flight test hangar during construction in December 1952. This aircraft crashed at Karachi on 3 March 1953 during its delivery flight. (*DH Photo*)

However, the first year of commercial jet airliner flying with BOAC was marred by the loss with all aboard Comet 1 G-ALYV on 2 May 1953 after taking off from Calcutta, bound for London. After take-off, at around 10,000 feet, the aircraft entered a violent storm resulting in high structural loads, causing the aircraft to break up, killing all thirty-seven passengers and six crew. This accident highlighted the need for weather radar, which had not been developed then, and no aircraft could be expected to withstand the stresses in such turbulent conditions. Therefore, the Comet did not display any inherent structural weakness.

Another BOAC Comet 1 was lost in mysterious circumstances when G-ALYP took off from Rome on 10 January 1954 and came down into the sea off Elba, killing twenty-nine passengers and six crew. On the following day, BOAC (in consultation with de Havilland) suspended Comet operations to allow detail checks to be made of the Comet fleet. As a result, some sixty precautionary modifications were made to the remaining aircraft, covering all suspected causes, allowing flying to recommence on 23 March. Then on 8 April 1954, again after take-off from Rome, Comet 1 G-ALYY was lost off Stromboli, resulting in an immediate grounding of all passenger-carrying Comets and the withdrawal of the certificate of airworthiness on 12 April, pending a full investigation into the cause.

A pioneering investigation commenced which involved for the first time the recovery of the wreckage of G-ALYP from the seabed, about 75 per cent of the aircraft being salvaged. All the parts were taken to the RAE at Farnborough where it was reassembled in a special rig to determine how it had broken up and therefore where the weak link was located. In parallel with this reconstruction, a fully instrumented Comet 1A G-ANAV was test flown from the RAE by John Cunningham and Roger Topp to check against the possibility of uncontrollable flutter of part of the structure causing a catastrophic failure. Comet 1 G-ALYU was installed in a water test tank at Farnborough with the wings out on both sides, where it was subjected to dynamic pressure testing and simulated flight loads until there was a failure in the cabin.

A court of inquiry was convened in London from 19 October until 24 November 1954 with the resulting report published on 12 February 1955. Although the structure had been designed to the highest standards established at the time, the pressure cabin had failed due to metal fatigue, which was established both from the recovered wreckage and the water tank testing, confirming that in addition to static structural testing, it was also vital to include dynamic testing. The areas of greatest stress were at the corners of the square cabin windows, where failure occurred, the actual stresses being much greater than anticipated, being in excess of 40,000 lb per square inch. With evidence gained from the Inquiry, not only was de

The water test tank at RAE Farnborough on 31 March 1955 with ex-BOAC Comet 1 G-ALYU being structurally tested. (*RAE Farnborough*)

Havilland able to redesign the Comet, but the world's aerospace industry was able to learn from the results. The de Havilland Aircraft Company was held in no way to blame, as the Comet had been designed to approved working practices based on the knowledge available at the time.

Meanwhile, although all Comet production had halted during the investigation and commercial operations ceased, development testing on the Comet 2 and the longer fuselage Comet 3 had continued. The Comet 3 was rolled out of the Experimental Department at Hatfield on 4 May 1954 ready for engine runs. The new aircraft was 18 feet longer than the Comet 1 with an AUW of 150,000 lb powered by four 10,000-lb thrust Avon jets. The Comet 3 featured rounded windows to smooth out the stresses, and while it was being prepared for flight, a second fuselage was installed in a water test tank for pressure proof testing.

G-ANLO was flown for the first time by John Cunningham on 19 July 1954 and had flown enough hours to qualify for its appearance at Farnborough in September. A recognition feature was wing leading edge pinion 856-gallon fuel tanks, taking total fuel capacity to 8,374 gallons. Development flying continued on Comet 2s, and with the delays caused by the investigation, a pair of more powerful Avon RA29 engines had become available, which was fitted in the outer nacelles of Comet 2s G-AMXD and G-AMXK for flight trials. Total sales at the time of the Comet Inquiry were 35 Comet 2s and eleven Comet 3s, including three to Pan American Airways.

BOAC did not take delivery of any Comet 2s for passenger operations, but with most featuring modified cabins with thicker skins and oval cabin windows, fourteen were eventually completed at Hatfield and another from Broughton, all apart from two going to the RAF. Three partially modified 2Rs were operated for intelligence gathering by 51 Squadron and ten fully modified Comet C.2s were flown worldwide by 216 Squadron from Lyneham. One ex-Air France Comet 1A survived to be preserved at the RAF Museum at Cosford, having had its cabin strengthened, and the original fuselage of Air France Comet 1A F-BGNX is preserved at the de Havilland Aircraft Museum in its original form with square windows.

The water tank at Hatfield with a modified Comet 2 test specimen being structurally tested for RAF operations. (*DH Photo*)

Comet 3 G-ANLO on pressure test at Hatfield on 5 May 1954 with the second fuselage beyond. (*DH Photo*)

de Havilland Propellers

When the de Havilland Propeller Company was incorporated in 1946, its core propeller business was declining following the massive design and production effort during the Second World War. Demand increased for propellers during the rearmament programme from 1950, but it was clear that a major diversification was required, using the skills and equipment available. The natural move was to take advantage in the upsurge of activity in the development of guided weapons.

The company engineers had gained experience with electronic methods of analysing the vibration characteristics of propellers to ensure efficiency and lightness with smooth running. A pair of 22 feet wide, 200 feet long propeller test tunnels had been completed at the end of 1946 at Hatfield, and the first propeller to be tested was for the Bristol Theseus, the first approved for a propeller turbine. By 1948, the company had managed to secure propeller business for all British transport aircraft produced since the end of the war, in addition to large transport aircraft with the RAF. The largest turbine propeller built anywhere in the world were the 16.5-foot eight-blade counter-rotating propellers for the Saunders-Roe Princess flying boat with a gross weight of 140 tons. However, there was production space available in the vast Second World War factory at Lostock which needed utilising, the company's registered offices being formally moved from Lostock to Hatfield in July 1953. One of the new challenges was the development of a hollow steel blade to maintain lightness for larger units. With overhaul life on modern propeller blades continuing to extend, service centres were set up globally and the overhaul base at Hatfield was moved to new premises at Stevenage in June 1955. The largest propeller developed by the company was a two-blade 80-foot diameter mounted on top of a 100-

foot tower in the Atlas Mountains 870 feet above sea level as the world's first wind generator, the turbine being capable of generating 100 kw.

The decision to enter the guided weapon business was made in 1951 with the company's experience in electronics, the initial work being the development of alternators for other manufacturers guided systems. By 1959, de Havilland Propeller alternators were fitted to most British guided weapons, with new accelerometer and miniature rate gyro introduced late in the same year. In addition, Propeller Company engineers were diversifying into systems in civil and military aerospace, as well as in other industries.

In the weapons field, de Havilland Propellers were contracted in April 1952 to develop an infrared homing head, resulting in bringing all the expertise together to develop a complete air-to-air missile initially called Blue Jay, but later named Firestreak. It was going to be most effective for the company to integrate the complete missile system, buying in the specialist propulsion and warhead expertise. Infrared guidance was a passive system which could not be detected by a target aircraft, the missile homing head seeking the target by the hot exhaust from the jet engine, the warhead being detonated by a close proximity fuse.

Only three years after starting the design, the first fully guided firing was made at Larkhill in 1954, impacting close to target centre from a range of several thousand yards. The Lostock factory was prepared for production to start in 1957, while a missile systems team was built up both at Hatfield and Lostock. The first air trials to check safe separation from a Venom by Des de Villiers, the Propeller Company chief test pilot. Initial ground launch trials were made from Pendine Sands in South Wales, the aircraft jacked up with its nose pointing out to sea. A test round was launched from a Venom over the Aberporth range off the Welsh coast, without a target, the performance recorded by ground-based telemetry. Following further airborne test launches, the first guided Firestreak was launched against a Firefly target aircraft fitted with a heat source to simulate a modern jet fighter, which was shot down into the sea from a test Venom by Mike Kilburn, the new chief test pilot.

Due to limitations on the Aberporth range, further trials were conducted at Woomera in Australia from early 1955, where conditions were much improved. Standard production Firestreaks were used by the RAF and RN Joint Service Trials Unit (JSTU) bringing the system up to a service standard. In less than seven years an entirely new form of sophisticated, lethal and reliable air-to-air weapon had been developed for the services, which could be fired from any modern fighter, detect a target from long range, follow it without any input from the pilot, and destroy the target despite any efforts at evasion. The only defence was to eject a heat source

Above left: Propeller final assembly and inspection. (*HS Photo*)

Above right: Contra-rotating propeller assembly for the Saunders Roe Princess flying boat, 29 December 1950. (*DH Photo*)

The sole flying Saunders Roe prototype (G-ALUN) fitted with de Havilland propellers. (*DH Photo*)

Propeller test cell on the Manor Road site at Hatfield, 6 January 1948. (*DH Photo*)

from the target aircraft simulating high engine heat at precisely the right moment. A drawback was that infrared systems could not be effective in heavy rain or cloud, but enemy nuclear bombers were expected to be at high altitude well above cloud. In 1958 and 1959, Firestreak was adopted as the air-to-air armament for all the main RAF and FAA fighters, including Lightnings, Javelins, and Sea Vixens.

An announcement was made in October 1958 that development was in hand for the development of a missile with superior performance to the Firestreak, which became Red Top. This was an all-aspect air-to-air missile that could detect kinetic airframe heat caused by high-speed airflow over the aircraft, avoiding the tail chase performance of Firestreak. This missile went on to arm later marks of the above three fighters.

In 1960, the de Havilland companies were merged into the Hawker Siddeley Group as part of the government policy to consolidate the British aerospace industry. The de Havilland Propeller Company became Hawker Siddeley Dynamics, which continued with missile system developments.

Towards the end of the 1960s, there was a requirement for a medium-range air-to-air missile, developed from the Raytheon AIM-7 Sparrow missile, which when fitted with an inverse monopulse semi-active radar-

Sea Vixen FAW.1 XJ481 from the pre-production development batch used for Firestreak air-to-air missile development at Woomera, Australia, painted white overall with diagonal matt black, being towed at Hatfield. The radar in the nose was replaced by cameras to record results of tests. (*Author's collection*)

The first Sea Vixen conversion to Mk 2 standard (XN684) was used for Red Top air-to-air missile development. (*DH Photo*)

homing seeker becoming the Skyflash, developed jointly by Hawker Siddeley Dynamics and Marconi Space and Defence Systems. An air staff requirement was issued in January 1972, and major changes to the Sparrow, in addition to the radar seeker, were improved electronics, adapted control surfaces and a Thorn EMI active radar fuse. Missile tests showed it could function in a hostile electronic countermeasures (ECM) environment with the capability of engaging targets under a wide variety of conditions. The missile entered service with the RAF in Phantoms in 1978, which in 1985 were replaced by Skyflash-armed Tornado F.3s. Four missiles were carried in under-fuselage recesses to reduce drag, both on the Phantom and Tornado. In RAF service, Skyflash was carried in conjunction with four Sidewinders, later replaced by ASRAAMs, the medium-range system replaced by AMRAAM from 1998 until retiring from service in 2002.

In addition to developing air-to-air weapons, engineers at the Manor Road site were also involved in the Anglo-French Martel anti-radiation missile. Martel was produced in two forms: one radar-guided (ARM) headed by the French, and the British-developed TV-guided version. Martel was a low-level anti-ship weapon with a long-range and powerful warhead. While France only used the radar-guided version, Britain used both types, typically with three TV or four ARM missiles on a Buccaneer from October 1972, and two carried by French Air Force Jaguars. The TV missile was guided to its target by the Buccaneer navigator, and once launched, the aircraft could turn for home, while the missile continued to its target.

Martel fuselage formed the basis for the turbojet-powered Sea Eagle long-range anti-ship missile, with the new missile being capable of launch from any aircraft able to fire Martel. Design of Sea Eagle commenced in 1976, followed by full-scale development in 1979, the new missile having a longer body, larger wings, and totally different internal systems when compared with Martel. Production started in 1982 with test firings up to 1984 ready for service introduction the next year. Once launched, Sea Eagle was completely autonomous with navigation and target seeking controlled by an on-board computer system. To increase the effect, an attack could be from multiple strike aircraft with missiles approaching from many directions against a hostile capital ship. Sea Eagle was introduced to the RAF on Buccaneers, followed by FAA Sea Harriers, and was used to arm Tornado GR.1s when they replaced Buccaneers, the missile being withdrawn from both the RAF and FAA by 2000.

Towards the end of 1993, demolition had commenced on the Manor Road site with the smashing of the structures resounding, destroying so many buildings that had contributed to the pioneer development of jet engines, propellers, and guided missiles. What missile development remained had been moved to Stevenage under the joint organisation of MBDA.

Sea Vixen FAW.2 XN686, incorrectly marked as XN685, carrying a Martel seeker head (TV guidance version) 9 June 1970, used for 'cat and mouse' trials. (*Author's collection*)

10

Blue Streak

The de Havilland Blue Streak liquid-propelled rocket project was conceived in the early 1950s as a nuclear deterrent delivery system. The German V2 rocket and American nuclear bombs on Japan had created two new technologies that were being developed into weapons by both the USA and USSR. The British Government decided that to remain an independent power, it also needed a nuclear deterrent for the RAF, and in June 1953, it issued operational requirement OR1139 for a ground-launched medium-range ballistic missile (MRBM) with extreme accuracy, carrying a thermo-nuclear warhead over a range of several thousand miles. To make the missile less vulnerable to destruction, it was to be launched from an underground silo, which was capable of withstanding a 1-MT atomic bomb ground burst at 1,000 yards.

The contract was not put out to tender, as it was considered that de Havilland success with the Firestreak and experience with pressurised aircraft was a natural choice to be the prime contractor. Contracts were awarded in great secrecy to de Havilland Propellers (DHP) for the missile and Rolls-Royce for engine development. Inertial guidance was the responsibility of Sperry, and Marconi was to develop the back-up radio guidance system. Overall project responsibility for managing the programme was with Royal Aircraft Establishment (RAE) at Farnborough, supported by other government agencies. The first launch was programmed during 1960 from Woomera in Australia.

Under the terms of an agreement with the USA, Britain was allowed access to American technology, with information supplied to de Havilland from Convair at San Diego, who were responsible for the Atlas programme. Although there was a major benefit from the Convair expertise following general principles, Blue Streak was launched with two rocket engines, while Atlas had three, and the smaller Blue Streak varied considerably from Atlas due to totally different requirements.

A government review of the programme was ordered in the autumn of 1959. The results on 23 December concluded that Blue Streak would only be effective as a first response by a Soviet attack with conventional weapons and would only have a limited retaliatory capability. The study group also concluded that only a mobile air- or submarine-launched nuclear weapon would be effective in all circumstances and in the long term. If satisfactory mutual arrangements could not be made with the USA, Blue Streak should continue in development, or it should be cancelled with the gap in Britain's nuclear weapon capability accepted. There was strong opposition to the concept of the perceived vulnerability of fixed-point launchers, with additional pressure from the Treasury, resulting in the government cancelling the project on 13 April 1960, and DHP being forced to declare over 1,000 highly skilled engineers redundant. After much discussion, an agreement was reached to maintain a reduced Blue Streak team to work on a satellite launcher programme, although the urgency was removed from the military programme. However, an experienced engineering capability was maintained to concentrate on a successful satellite launch vehicle.

In the late 1950s, combined design studies by de Havilland Propellers and the RAE concentrated on converting Blue Streak from a weapon system, to be fitted with the Saunders-Roe-developed Black Knight, which would be capable of launching a small payload into space. Further studies showed Black Arrow, a development of Black Knight, could launch an even larger satellite, which was sized to fit on the top of Blue Streak. The government considered the development of a space launch capability was beyond the capability of Britain, but the cancellation of Blue Streak as a weapon made a considerable amount of materials and facilities that could be used in a space programme available.

Peter Thorneycroft, minister of aviation, made proposals to reluctant France, Germany, and Italy, which resulted in the formation of the European Launcher Development Organisation (ELDO) with the HQ in Paris. In the end, the French agreed to develop the second stage, the Germans the third stage, and Italy the fairing and dummy satellite, with Blue Streak as the first stage. Australia agreed to provide the launch facilities and each country was responsible for its own contribution, the entire project gaining the title Europa. With Blue Streak in an advanced stage, well ahead of the other contributions, it was decided to launch the first three vehicles as single stages. Each Blue Streak was assembled at Stevenage and statically tested at Spadeadam, before shipping to Australia for launch, the first being launched successfully on 5 June 1964. The first Europa with dummy upper stages was launched on 24 May 1966.

During the 1960s, there were ten launches from Woomera, with varying degrees of success from upper stages, while Blue Streak behaved as planned and met the mission requirements. Woomera was not the ideal launch site as it was too far from the equator to maximise the effect of the earth's rotation for placing payloads into orbit. The French therefore proposed moving the launch site to Kourou in French Guiana, just 5 degrees from the equator. A new launcher was manufactured, which was installed at Kourou by an Australian team in the launch facility prepared by the French. The final launch from Woomera with three stages was in June 1970 and was nearly successful, but the fairing did not detach from the third stage, resulting in the stage and fairing with the satellite inside re-entering the atmosphere over the Caribbean without completing an earth orbit. In 1972, vehicle number eleven was the first and only Blue Streak to be launched from Kourou, and although Blue Streak once again performed well, it did not receive the correct signals from the guidance system located in an upper stage, allowing the vehicle to wander off course and destroying itself before second-stage separation.

Britain became an observer in ELDO in 1968 and stopped funding after 1973. The French went on to lead the Ariane launch vehicle for Europe under the organisation of the European Space Agency (ESA), which was set up in 1973, while the British government decided to rely on American vehicles as launchers for British satellites, an industry in which Britain has become highly successful, with headquarters in the original de Havilland factory in Stevenage, now operated by Airbus Defence and Space. Blue Streak was an outstanding technical success but suffered from a lack of government commitment and long-term investment.

The structures were assembled by de Havilland Aircraft at Hatfield in wartime Mosquito Repair Organisation (MRO) buildings by the boundary with the Barnet Bypass, A1 Great North Road. Although the project was highly classified, little local interest was shown, and it was unofficially known as the 'special tank department', but within de Havilland, it was 'Project 3000'. Details and sub-assemblies were produced in the specialised departments in the factory or sourced from sub-contractors. A basic design was agreed between RAE Farnborough and DHP, with structural design the responsibility of de Havilland Aircraft. Systems design incorporation was by an engineering team based in Conquest House in London, where the requirements of a very urgent programme had to be met, requiring a close liaison between the Hatfield and London teams, although due to the fast-changing requirements, there was confusion from time to time.

Blue Streak assembly in the Project 3000 building at Hatfield. (*DH Photo*)

Raising the pressurised space frame of the Blue Streak into the vertical position in the tower alongside the Barnet Bypass at Hatfield. (*DH Photo*)

The vehicle was designed in four sections consisting of a propulsion bay, fuel tank bay, guidance bay, and transition bay with provision for a dummy warhead for the early development models. For the subsequent satellite launch vehicle, the guidance bay was replaced by an equipment bay and small transition bay to match the second stage. In the propulsion bay, two Rolls-Royce RZ2 rocket engines were suspended from main thrust beams fitted across the bay, the beam ends projecting from the sides of the skin to provide hold down points for the overall vehicle when on the launch pad. This bay was made from conventional aircraft aluminium alloy structure, supported by frames and skin stringers.

The tank bay structure was made from an argon arc-welded stainless sheet on horizontal rollers, the tank being in two parts, separated by a hemispherical dome. The upper section containing liquid oxygen was an unsupported balloon structure, relying on air pressure for its stability due to the thinness of the lightweight skin. The lower section contained fuel and was reinforced by stringers spot welded at the joints. Hemispherical stainless-steel domes closed each end of the tanks. Once structural complete, the tank section was pressurised and raised in a cradle to the vertical position for leak and pressure testing in water in a special test tower erected close to the fence with the A1 road, which became a prominent landmark. Once manufactured, the unpressurised tank required an end load of 16,000 lb applied along its axis to stabilise the structure. The guidance bay was also of stainless construction with access panels for servicing systems that were more vibration-sensitive at the front end of the vehicle where there was a more benign environment.

Final assembly and equipping were undertaken at Stevenage, on a site originally built as a machine shop for the Comet, later used for propeller overhauls. Structures were supplied from Hatfield on special stands for assembly with each bay equipped and tested electrically as well as for pipework leaks, ready for assembly. Once assembly was complete, Blue Streak was delivered on its dedicated road trailer to its allocated test site. Additional facilities were constructed on the Manor Road side of the airfield for propellant flow testing and also checking launcher release gear separation. Among the structures erected was a tower where the missile could simulate a launch by using a hydraulic ram to lift the vehicle 10 inches clear, but no motors were fired despite some pyrotechnic effects when surplus fuel was burned off. The site was erected in the late 1950s and finally cleared in 1973. All static firings of Blue Streak in the UK were on the Spadeadam ranges in Cumbria where considerable facilities were constructed, managed by Rolls-Royce.

Blue Streak was designed and built using adapted aerospace technology, creating an all-new space capability, which was later to become a very

The Blue Streak test site off Manor Road at Hatfield. The main tower was used to check separation of all the connectors at the initial stage of launch. (*DH Photo*)

Static firing of Europa I, formally Blue Streak, at Spadeadam near Carlisle, Cumbria. (*HS Photo*)

The launch of Europa I F/6 from Woomera Range in Australia. (*HS Photo*)

successful satellite business, which still exists today. The reliability required for a nuclear weapon, in safety terms, needed to be developed, and when it became a potential satellite launcher, reliability was essential for both safety and commercial requirements. Blue Streak never suffered a major failure, either during testing or in flight, confirming the new ways of working were valid. One of the most significant steps was the use of cleanrooms for manufacture, required to stop contamination of the propellant and the complete absence of oil or grease on any surface in contact with liquid oxygen, which could lead to catastrophic failure. Stainless steel needed to be welded to a very high specification, with only one man—Ernie Gray—achieving the required standards, contributing to the majority of in-house welding.

A total of eighty-eight trials took place over thirteen years from 1960, and although the project was full of risks, no serious accidents occurred. Now, little remains of Blue Streak, apart from an example in the National Space Museum in Leicester and one stored at the Scottish Museum of Flight.

11

DH 110 and Sea Vixen

Following positive experience with Vampire FAA operations, it was decided to investigate the feasibility of an advanced all-weather jet fighter with twin-engined security, initial discussions taking place in 1946 between de Havilland and the Admiralty, resulting in the proposal for what became the DH 110. A twin-boom layout was retained to allow easier carrier stowage, and keeping the engines close together avoided asymmetric control problems in the event of an engine failure. Following results from the DH 108 research programme, a 40-degree swept-back wing was chosen, with provision for wing folding to allow lowering on deck lifts and reduce stowage space. The proposed armament was four of the new 30-mm Aden cannons. A unique feature was the pilot's cockpit offset to port, with the observer buried in the fuselage under a flush hatch on the starboard side in semi-darkness to overcome the dimness of early AI radars.

In January 1947, Naval Spec. 40/46 and RAF Spec. F.44/46 were issued to cover the basic requirements for a night fighter, with de Havilland offering the DH 110 for both specifications. Greater interest was shown by the RAF, with an updated Spec. F.4/48 issued in February 1948, so the Ministry of Supply placed orders in April 1949 to de Havilland for seven land-based night fighters and two long-range fighter prototypes for the RAF, plus two of each night fighter prototypes and strike fighter prototypes for the Fleet Air Arm to Spec. N.14/49. Meanwhile, as an RAF insurance, four prototypes of the competing delta wing Gloster GA 5 night fighter were also ordered.

As an example of the advanced nature of the programme at the time, the RAF requirement was for a night fighter capable of intercepting hostile aircraft up to 40,000 feet, with a maximum speed of at least 525 kt at 25,000 feet, and it had to be capable of reaching its service ceiling of 45,000 feet in no more than ten minutes. It needed to carry sufficient fuel for an endurance of two hours, including a climb to 25,000 feet with fifteen minutes of combat and the remainder cruising on patrol. Provision was to be made for the carriage of underwing drop tanks to further increase the range. A very rapid take-off was required, in the most ten seconds, but five seconds was more desirable, without additional assistance of catapults or rockets. Take-off distance was to be 1,500 yards, with landing distance 1,200 yards over an imaginary 50-foot barrier. While flying at top speed at sea level, the airframe had to be able to withstand up to 4 g loads while manoeuvring in combat. The pressure cabin was to be able to reproduce the altitude pressure of 25,000 feet at a ceiling of 45,000 feet, the workload being such that two crew would be required and provided with ejection seats. Production totals were estimated to be 150 aircraft at the rate of ten per month, and simple and rapid servicing was essential for rapid turn round between sorties.

In November 1949, for financial and political reasons, the FAA selected the simpler and more readily available Sea Venom to replace Sea Hornets, while the RAF order was reduced to prototypes each of the DH 110 and GA 5, seriously delaying the development of both types, resulting in the introduction of interim types to fill the resulting gap. The two prototype DH 110s were built in the Experimental Department at Hatfield with power coming from a pair of 7,500-lb thrust Rolls-Royce Avon RA.7 turbojets. The first flight of WG236 was made from Hatfield by John Cunningham on 26 September 1951, just too late for the Farnborough air show that year. During the flight development programme, it exceeded the speed of sound in a shallow dive on 9 April 1952 and was joined by the black painted second prototype WG240 on 25 July 1952.

Just over a month later, the first prototype made its public debut at the Farnborough Air Show, but it disintegrated on 6 September when flying fast and low towards the crowd, killing John Derry and Tony Richards, the engines separating with one falling in the crowd, killing twenty-nine spectators and injuring many others. On investigation, it was found the disintegration was caused by the torsional failure of the wing during a combined acceleration and rate of roll, the leading-edge wing skins becoming detached and peeled back. The SBAC amended the flying rules, banning all flying towards the spectators—a common-sense rule that is now in operation at all air shows. The grounded second prototype was modified with a reinforced wing structure and revised tail outline, and when test flying was recommenced, it became the first British aircraft with an all-moving tail.

First prototype DH 110 (WG236), which was flown for the first time by John Cunningham on 26 September 1951 and exceeded the speed of sound in a shallow dive on 9 April 1952. (*DH Photo*)

John Derry and Tony Richards, who were killed when DH 110 WG236 crashed at the Farnborough Air Show on 6 September 1952. (*DH Photo*)

With the loss of RAF interest in the DH 110, the Gloster GA 5 was ordered into super priority production as the Javelin land-based all-weather fighter, despite problems with accidents and a challenging development programme, leaving the future for the DH 110 rather bleak. However, the FAA still had a requirement for a high-performance, all-weather strike fighter, and in 1952, a requirement was published for a Sea Venom replacement. A swept wing Venom known as the DH 116 was studied but shelved in favour of an updated DH 110, the development continuing under a naval contract, with the new aircraft bearing a superficial resemblance to the original design powered by two increased-power Avon engines, increased fuel capacity, and the full range of naval modifications. The four cannons were retained in the early stages as a secondary armament, but the primary armament was to be Blue Jay, later to become Firestreak infrared-homing air-to-air missiles. For the first time, de Havilland was becoming involved in the development of a complete weapon system, rather an aircraft with stores attached. The surviving second prototype was delivered to A&AEE Boscombe Down in September 1954 in preparation for deck trials, which were completed as a series of touch and go landings on HMS *Albion* on 23 September by Lt Cdr Jock Elliott; although the undercarriage was strengthened, no arrester hook was fitted.

Development continued with the order in February 1954 for a semi-navalised DH 110 prototype Mk 20X XF828, which was built at the old Airspeed factory at Christchurch with W. A. (Bill) Tamblin leading the design team. More powerful Rolls-Royce Avon 208 turbojets developing 11,230-lb thrust each were installed, and arrester gear and long stroke undercarriage were fitted, but there was no radar or folding wings with this aircraft. The first flight was from Christchurch to Hurn on 20 June 1955 by Jock Elliott, who was by then in charge of the DH 110 flight development programme. The first deck landings were carried out on HMS *Ark Royal* on 5 April 1956 by Cdr S. G. Orr, the programme including unassisted and steam catapult take-offs and arrested landings under all operational conditions.

Finally, the long-delayed production order was placed in January 1955 for a total of seventy-eight DH 110s, including a batch of twenty-one pre-production aircraft to be used in the development programme of the new weapon system, leading quickly to service entry. The airframe was about 80 per cent redesigned to Spec. N.139P, the major changes including power-folding wings, a new pilot cockpit canopy, catapult pick-up points, steerable nosewheel and the latest AI radar under a pointed nose radome, which could be folded sideways to reduce aircraft length. The fixed cannons were deleted, making the DH 110 the first British jet fighter not to be armed with guns, the primary armament being four Firestreaks carried on underwing pylons. For ground attack duties, twenty-eight 2-inch rocket unguided projectiles could be launched from a retractable ventral pack forward of the nosewheel. Additional war loads such as bombs, rocket packs, or fuel tanks could be carried on underwing pylons.

On 5 March 1957, the DH 110 was officially named Sea Vixen FAW.20, later amended to FAW.1 and the first production aircraft XJ474 was rolled off the Christchurch production line in February 1957, making its first flight on 20 March. It was positioning to the flight development base at Hurn, where the airfield was more suited for testing high-performance aircraft. Production of Sea Vixens ceased at Christchurch with the 118th aircraft in August 1962, with the line moving to Broughton where a last Mk 1 was built, followed by twenty-nine FAW.2s, the last one flying on 3 February 1966. With the overall development programme completed, there were intensive service trials with 700Y Flight at Yeovilton using eight Sea Vixen FAW.1s. This unit was reformed and commissioned on 2 July 1959 as 892 NAS, embarking on HMS *Ark Royal* on 3 March 1960. This was followed by 890, 893, and 899 NAS, while training was the responsibility of 766 NAS.

With Sea Vixen FAW.1s established in service, de Havilland began to study a range of improvements to increase range and performance, but by the early 1960s, a more conservative programme was adopted, which visually included pinion fuel tanks on the front of the tail booms, and missile armament changed to the improved Red Top with the tail boom fairings increased in size to accommodate additional avionics. Two FAW.1s (XN684 and XN685) were flown off the production line at Christchurch and converted into FAW.2 development aircraft in the Experimental Department, with design responsibility now returned to Hatfield. Chris Capper, the Sea Vixen project pilot, flew XN684 on 1 June 1962; when joined by the second aircraft, they were allocated to Red Top trials at Hatfield and Boscombe Down, joining a number of other Sea Vixens based with de Havilland Propellers at Hatfield.

In addition to the new build FAW.2s at Broughton, many of the FAW.1s were also converted to FAW.2 standard. The first production FAW.2 (XP919) was flown from Hawarden on 8 March 1963 and based at Hatfield for performance trials in 1964, later joining 766 NAS. The withdrawal of Sea Vixens from service commenced with the disbandment of 892 NAS in October 1968 in preparation for the service entry of the Phantom FG.1, with 899 NAS finally disbanding on 23 January 1972 as the final Sea Vixen front-line unit.

The Sea Vixen therefore closed the de Havilland jet fighter era, and although it failed to achieve an RAF order instead of the Gloster Javelin, it remained in front-line service longer than the Javelin as an effective strike fighter, as well as being capable of a rapid climb to 40,000 feet where it could outmanoeuvre many interceptors.

12

Comet 4

As well as learning lessons from the Comet accident investigation, in the intervening period, developments had taken place which outdated the stretched Comet 3. The pressure cabin needed to be built using a thicker-gauge, fatigue-resistant aluminium alloy, and production techniques had to be improved drastically. Where skins had previously been countersunk for flush riveting, the skin was spin dimpled to retain strength without removing material. On 17 March, de Havilland announced its programme for a new world airliner known as the Comet 4, with a launch order from BOAC for nineteen aircraft, plus a structural test airframe. Although aerodynamically similar to the Comet 3, the fuselage was redesigned, fuel capacity was increased to 8,750 gallons, and power was to be from four 10,500-lb thrust Rolls-Royce RA29 Avon turbojets. The aircraft range gave typical stage lengths of 2,870 miles, achieving London to Johannesburg with two intermediate stops. The Comet 4 was planned to enter service in 1958, the Comet 3 having been used to provide performance and aerodynamic data, saving time with the Comet 4 development programme. The all-up weight of the Comet 4 was 152,500 lb with a payload of 16,850 lb, the new Avons giving a very spirited take-off performance; cruising speed was Mach 0.74, equivalent to 489 mph.

The cabin could carry up to seventy-six passengers, five abreast at 38-inch pitch, and it was possible to fly the 3,502 miles from London to New York with one refuelling stop. The crew was two pilots, a flight engineer, and navigator. With further testing, it was expected performance figures would improve, allowing London to Johannesburg with only one stop in an elapsed time of thirteen hours. The Comet 4 did not have a full non-stop London to New York capacity, but to achieve this would require a larger aircraft, which would be too large for average global routes.

By mid-1955, the major Comet 4 design was complete, and building the aircraft commenced at Hatfield, including a comprehensive structural static and dynamic test programme. The Comet 3 prototype had also been fitted with Avon RA29s, achieving some 80 per cent of the certificate of airworthiness flying to be completed before the maiden flight of the Comet 4. In order to gain operational experience for the Comet 4, Comet 3 G-ANLO was flown by John Cunningham, with Peter Bugge as his deputy and Peter Cane from BOAC on the first round the world flight by a jet airliner. The departure was from Hatfield on 2 December 1955 heading for Sydney via Cairo, Bombay, Singapore, and Darwin, arriving at Sydney after twenty-four hours and twenty-four minutes of flying time. Flying back across the Pacific, the aircraft returned to Heathrow on 28 January after flying some 30,000 miles overall. During the flight, a number of demonstrations were made with a high level of reliability and regularity. For this jet pioneering achievement, John Cunningham was awarded the Harmon Trophy by the US president.

Meanwhile, a new pressure test tank had been commissioned at Hatfield to simulate a flight every four minutes. The first test specimen was a strengthened Comet 2 airframe, which started fatigue testing on 26 November 1955, with the fuselage immersed in the tank and the wings protruding out each side through water seals to simulate flight loads. The tank was long enough to accommodate a Comet 4 fuselage, but initially the shorter Comet 2 cabin was tested for the RAF, with production-standard Comet 4 fuselage sections also tested prior to the installation of the complete new airframe. The tests simulated flights with full pressurisation in the cabin, and flight loads simulated on the wings and tail. The tests were run round the clock for forty-eight hours, simulating 1,500 hours flying time, the tank being emptied for airframe inspection, before repeating the test again and again. The aim of the programme was to demonstrate the airframe could withstand 60,000 reversals without any fatigue crack appearing in the structure, and any subsequent cracks would be contained for another 60,000 reversals, giving an overall safe life of 30,000 flying hours.

In mid-1957, de Havilland released initial details of the shorter-range continental Comet 4B, which offered jet speed and comfort for similar costs to existing propeller turbine airliners. Increased capacity in a stretched fuselage made room for up to ninety-nine passengers (a 10 per cent increase over the Comet 4), giving a 15 per cent reduction in seat–mile costs over stages of between 300 and 2,000 miles. British European Airways (BEA), now part of British Airways, ordered an initial batch of six Comet 4Bs with 100 seats to be used on the longer Mediterranean routes. The Comet 3 prototype (G-ANLO) had its outer wings replaced

Above: Comet 3 G-ANLO pushed out of the Experimental Department on 5 May 1954 with de Havilland Propellers in the background. (*DH Photo*)

Left: Comet 3 G-ANLO on stop-over at Hawaii during the first round the world flight by a jet airliner. (*DH Photo*)

by shorter span extension wings without the pinion fuel tanks, designated Comet 3B as part of the flight test programme for the new variant. At the end of 1957, the ultimate Comet 4C was announced, combining the longer fuselage of the Comet 4B with the long-range wings of the Comet 4, carrying eighty-five passengers over stages of 2,475 miles, this version becoming the major export version.

By the spring of 1958, Comet 4 production was well established at Hatfield, with a second production line created at Broughton. The Comet 4 was an excellent example of how de Havilland took basic raw materials delivered to the factory and created a very sophisticated global jet airliner largely within the Hatfield site. Avon engines were delivered from Rolls-Royce, avionics, and instrumentation from specialist companies, but most of the remainder was fabricated at Hatfield. Behind the main administration building, which is now a police HQ, the main factory had two passages leading towards the production line. Down 'A' passage, on the left, were the main stores, and on the right was production control. Moving down the passage, on the right was the fitting shop where details were manufactures and fitted together. At a crossroads of the passage, to the right was metal form, where either drop hammers gradually formed panels, while others were stretch formed over coated concrete moulds. Going straight on at the crossroads, on the right was upholstery, with electrical sub-assemble (ESA) opposite. Upholstery was where bulkheads were trimmed, galleys constructed, and cabin trim prepared using fibreglass moulded in the plastics department. ESA made up wiring looms

Comet 4B G-ANLO in BEA markings with reduced wing span and pinion fuel tanks removed. The integral air traffic control tower is behind on the corner of the flight test hangar. (*DH Photo*)

and connected up electrical panels prior to assembly in the aircraft. In the opposite direction to metal form was a machine shop, supplemented by another machine shop in a nearby building. Hydraulic and pneumatic pipes were made up in the coppersmiths and sheet metal department, also on the aerodrome.

At this point, the main assembly area was located, the first department being sub-assembly (SAD) where control surfaces, access doors, tailplanes, and fins were built. To the far left were treatment tanks for degreasing and applying surface finishes. Also nearby was a detail paint shop. Beyond SAD (where Mosquito production was during the Second World War) was the Comet wing shop, where on the right, Comet inner wing sections including the engine fairings, and extension wings were assembled in pits with access top and bottom. When a set was complete, it was moved along the line to the left, to the wing centre-section jig, where the wing roots were drilled on assembly to ensure a perfect fit, and four bolts cooled in nitrogen were put in the reamed holes, expanding as they warmed up to a tight fit.

During the training with the de Havilland Aeronautical School, the author spent some time in the Comet wing shop, working with fitter Tom Jevens, installing fuel pipes inside the 'wet wing' integral fuel tanks, to feed fuel from the outer wing and pinion tanks. Access was through an opened lower-skin sealed manhole and crawling through various gaps where the ribs sections had been temporarily removed. Crawling around with a lead lamp, tools, and parts over the stiffeners in a Bostik sealant atmosphere made more comfortable with corrugated cardboard was probably against all modern health and safety regulations.

Superintendent of the wing shop was Bill Mallon, a veteran of Mosquito production, and his assistant was Stan Wright. The superintendent of the erecting shop was Jock Harrison, and we were located in the offices dividing the wing and erecting shops. For anyone who is familiar with the classic movie *Sound Barrier*, during the scene in the factory where Comet 1s are being built, the stairs were the ones I went up, but in my case, they did not open out into Ralph Richardson's splendid panelled office with bookcases and a cocktail cabinet.

Meanwhile, in another part of the site was the 'Comet fuse shop' located in the old Second World War flying school. With steel rail tracks in the floor, the fuselage sections were brought together with stringers Redux bonded to the skins and flush riveted around the frames. There was a flat pressure bulkhead forward of the flight deck, to which would be fitted weather radar under a radome. The rear cabin had a pressure dome with the unpressurised rear fuselage aft supporting the tail units. When complete, the fuselage would be pressure-tested to ensure no leaks and transported to the start of the production line. where it came through a large side door.

The main production line, separated from the wing shop by offices, was also used for Mosquito Second World War production; it had a relatively low roof clearance, with areas where a fin and rudder would be clear. Fuselage and wing assembly started at the left-hand end, the first Comet 4 (G-APDA) being at the start of the line. Following main assembly and undercarriage installation, the rear fuselage was ballasted and lowered to allow the aircraft to be pulled backwards down the line to the high bay at the end where engines could be fitted, systems installation completed, and the aircraft painted. All Comet 4s built at Hatfield went through this process, with work including fitting out of the flight deck and the furnishing of the cabin, complete with bought out passenger seats.

In early February 1958, G-APDA had its engines installed and resonance testing to check for flutter in the experimental department. This was followed by engine runs and compass swing ready for John Cunningham and crew to take it aloft on 27 April 1958, the start of the flight development programme, much of which had been achieved with the Comet 3.

The first export sale was announced on 19 March 1958 for six Comet 4s to be operated by Aerolineas Argentinas. Meanwhile, two Comet 2Es each with a pair of RA29 engines in the outer positions had been undertaking Avon certification and endurance testing. Comet 4 G-APDA was involved in a number of overseas proving flights, one being the opening of the new 7,730 feet runway at Hong Kong (Kai Tak Airport on 12 September 1958), making the 7,925-mile return flight to London in three stages via Bombay and Cairo with an elapsed time of eighteen hours and twenty-two minutes. The Comet had also been flown into New York's Idlewild Airport (now Kennedy Airport) on 11 August by John Cunningham to check compliance with noise regulations, returning to Hatfield in the unofficial record time of six hours and sixteen minutes.

From 16 to 22 September, G-APDA made a sales tour of Canada and South America, flying 23,000 miles, including a full load take off from 7,340 feet elevation Mexico City to Lima, using the 8,200 feet secondary runway as the main one was out of use.

On 30 September 1958, the first two Comet 4s were handed over to BOAC at Heathrow Airport, with a third aircraft arriving on 3 October, poised to restart commercial jet airliner operations. Although the Comet 4 was intended for BOAC empire routes to African and Asia, a spectacular start was made by BOAC, inaugurating the world's first jet transatlantic service from London to New York on 2 October 1958, followed by regular services from 4 October, becoming a daily service from 14 November. This beat the PanAm Boeing 707 services by five weeks.

In late summer 1958, East African Airways ordered two, later increased to three Comet 4s to the same specification as BOAC, with deliveries in 1960.

The first Comet 4 G-APDA for BOAC being pulled past the flight test hangar, incorporating air traffic control and the fire station. (*DH Photo*)

The all new Comet 4 G-APDA was first flown by John Cunningham on 27 April 1958 with the flight test hangar and erecting shop in the background. (*DH Photo*)

The first Comet 4 export order was for three aircraft to Aerolineas Argentinas; the first (LV-PLM) was delivered on 2 March 1959. (*DH Photo*)

The first two Comet 4s (G-APDB and G-APDC) handed over to BOAC at London Heathrow on 30 September 1958, with the first transatlantic jet service to New York on 4 October. (*DH Photo*)

From 1 April 1959, BOAC introduced Comet 4s on their intended routes from Europe to Asia, carrying double the passengers on stages twice as long as Comet 1s. The Comet 4 high power-to-weight ratio gave a dramatic take-off and climb performance from tropical runways, the Comet being able to operate from existing airports without any restrictions, resulting in regular schedules being maintained. The Comet was the right jet at the right time, ready to revolutionise travel standards and financial returns.

In the spring of 1959, the Comet fatigue test specimen passed the 100,000-hour mark, equivalent to thirty-three years of airline operations. The first delivery to Aerolineas Argentinas on 2 March 1959, and the first Comet 4B for BEA was rolled off the production line on 15 June 1959, entering regular service with the airline on 1 April 1960. Comet 4 production was added to Broughton with the fifth aircraft for BOAC (G-APDE) delivered on 2 October 1958, while Hatfield concentrated on Comet 4Bs, and Comet 4Cs were shared between the two factories. Comets at Broughton were built nose first, as there was adequate headroom for the tail. On 20 July 1959, Olympic Airways announced their intention to acquire two Comet 4Bs to the same specification as BEA.

On 30 October 1959, Mexicana (CMA) signed for three Comet 4Cs, the first customer for this version; the aircraft made its maiden flight from Hatfield the next day. In early 1960, Misrair—the national airline of Egypt and later to become United Arab Airlines (UAA)—ordered three Comet 4Cs, eventually taking a total of eight aircraft, the last one being the final Comet built when it was delivered on 26 February 1964. BEA eventually operated fourteen Comet 4Bs with Olympic taking four, working in close co-operation. Delivery of Comet 4 G-APDJ to BOAC on 11 January 1960 completed the total of nineteen aircraft in the fleet, only sixteen months from the initial delivery, all ahead of schedule. In January 1960, Middle East Airlines (MEA) ordered four Comet 4Cs to be based in Beirut. The last two airline customers for Comet 4Cs were two for Sudan Airways and two for Kuwait Airways. The second Comet 4C for Sudan (ST-AAX) was the last Hatfield-built Comet and had to be removed from the factory through side doors as the normal exit was blocked by the build-up of the newer Trident assembly. ST-AAX was delivered on 21 December 1962.

A unique VIP Comet 4C SA-R-7 was ordered by Saudi Arabian Airlines for the personal use of King Ibn Saud, the first of many jet airliner conversions for VIP use. The aircraft was built at Hatfield and had many special features, including a VIP front cabin and tourist seats in the rear cabin. The first flight from Hatfield was on 29 March 1962, followed by the first European flight in June. In August, the aircraft made its first visit to Jeddah, with crew training starting at Hatfield in late September through

BEA placed an initial order for six stretched Comet 4Bs with pinion fuel tanks not fitted. The first was G-APMA, delivered to the airline on 20 December 1959. (*DH Photo*)

Sudan Air Comet 4C ST-AAX was the last Comet to be built at Hatfield and had to be extricated through a side door in the erecting shop as the end was blocked by assembly of the first Trident. (*DH Photo*)

October including route proving around Europe and occasional visits to Saudi Arabia, but mainly based at Hatfield. By this time, the author had become PA to John Cunningham (the chief test pilot and Second World War night fighter ace with twenty successes), and SA-R-7 was my responsibility to administer, ensuring accommodation was booked for the crew and diplomatic clearances were obtained. The de Havilland crew was made up of test pilot John Hanslip and flight engineer Ken Rouse, and they were training an American crew seconded from TWA to take over the full operation of the aircraft.

On 19 March 1963, the aircraft was requested to fly from Hatfield to Geneva to commence a shuttle from Nice to Geneva with King Saud and his retinue on the first shuttle. On the third flight carrying the last of the passengers and luggage, the American crew were close to being cleared, and both John and Ken were resting in the rear of the aircraft after a long duty day. In the early hours of 20 March, the aircraft struck an Alpine ridge near Cuneo and all on board were killed.

BOAC withdrew its Comet 4s towards the end of 1965, the final commercial flight being with G-APDM from New Zealand to London on 24 November. Five of the aircraft were bought by Malaysian Airways— later to become Malaysia-Singapore Airlines (MSA)—while the majority of the remainder went to Dan-Air. BEA and Olympic began to withdraw Comet 4Bs in the spring of 1969, the last service being from Malaga to Heathrow on 31 October 1971 by G-APMA. Some Comet 4Bs were allocated to BEA Airtours based at Gatwick, continuing in operations

Comet 4Cs combined the stretched fuselage of the Comet 4B with the long-range wing of the Comet 4. Comet 4C SA-R-7 for King Saud of Saudi Arabia was the first large business jet, but it was lost in the Alps on 20 March 1963. (*Author's collection*)

until 31 January 1973. Channel Airways acquired five Comet 4Bs, but went into liquidation on 1 February 1972, the surviving aircraft joining the Dan-Air fleet either entering service on passenger charter operations or broken up for spares. Three of the four MEA Comet 4Cs were destroyed in the Israeli attack on Beirut Airport on 28 December 1968, the survivor going to Dan-Air for spares. Dan-Air progressively acquired Comets from EAA, MSA, Egyptair, Sudanair, and Kuwait Airways, making Dan-Air ultimately the largest Comet fleet operator.

The RAF was a major Comet operator, initially with Comet 2s, either already completed for BOAC or in an advanced stage of construction. Three of the earliest remained with unmodified cabins apart from some strengthening around the cabin windows allowing the cabin to be pressurised to 4 lb per square inch and were modified for Electronic Intelligence (ELINT) duties with various radomes and aerials fitted. These aircraft were flown by 192 Squadron based at Watton and later 51 Squadron from Wyton on intelligence gathering missions on the fringe of Iron Curtain countries.

In February 1955, the RAF placed an order for ten Comet 2s, the first two being T.Mk 2s for training, and the remainder to a full passenger-carrying capability as C Mk 2s, the initial aircraft being later completed to the passenger configuration. These aircraft had strengthened cabins with oval windows and other modifications to bring them up to a full civil certificate of airworthiness standard for high-speed worldwide passenger operations. On 7 and 8 June 1956, the first two Comets were delivered to 216 Squadron at Lyneham, the first official operation being a ministerial flight to Moscow for the Tushino Air Display on 24 June. Full-scale operations commenced in June 1957, supporting V-Bomber deployments, transport of troops and RN ships companies, as well as Royal Flights and Government ministers. The aircraft could also be configured in medical role with patients carried on a smooth, quiet and rapid transport home to Britain. Generally, thirty-six patients could be carried in a Comet 2 with six stretchers in the forward cabin, eight reclining seats in the rear cabin, and the remainder in standard trooping seats with a medical team and other passengers.

On 5 September 1960, de Havilland announced an order for five Comet 4Cs for RAF Transport Command designated C Mk 4s for delivery during 1961 and 1962. These aircraft were to operate alongside Comet C.2s all with 216 Squadron, the first aircraft making its maiden flight from Hawarden on 15 November 1961 and following a programme of crew training at Hatfield all were delivered to Lyneham by 1 June 1962. Comet 2s continued in service with 216 Squadron until March 1967, when XK698 made the final sortie. Comet 2Rs with 51 Squadron were withdrawn towards the end of 1974 when they were replaced by specially modified Nimrod R.1s.

Comet C.4s continued with 216 Squadron until disbandment on 30 June 1975, the final commemorative flight being made by XR395 from Lyneham over Heathrow and Hatfield to storage at Leconfield. All five aircraft were added to the Dan-Air fleet in early September 1975, and the aircraft were converted to civil operations at Lasham, continuing in service for another five years until the final commemorative flight on 9 November 1980.

When Comet production finished, there were still two Comet 4C airframes stored in the Broughton factory, and when the Comet-based Nimrod was ordered for maritime reconnaissance with the RAF, these two airframes were modified for the development programme. Both aircraft had their fuselages shortened to Comet 4 cabin length and the first, XV147 was flown from Hawarden to the Hawker Siddeley airfield at Woodford on 25 October 1965 for conversion to Nimrod configuration, flying again after conversion 31 July 1967 still powered by RA29 engines. The second aircraft (XV148) was converted at Broughton complete with Rolls-Royce Spey engines and made its first flight to Woodford on 23 May 1967, where all Nimrod development and production was located in the ex-Avro factory, where Lancaster and Vulcan bombers had been built.

One further Comet 4C was completed at Broughton as a flying laboratory for testing new equipment and navigation systems. Comet 4C XS235 first flew from Hawarden to Hatfield on 26 September 1963, where it was fitted out with a special interior consisting of racks and stations to undertake a range of experiments. Overall flying hours were low, as the aircraft was grounded for extended periods while new equipment and systems were installed and ground-tested before flight testing. This Comet named *Canopus* was delivered to Boscombe Down on 2 December 1963 where it was based with the radio and navigation department, and it was the last Comet to fly until its final landing at Bruntingthorpe on 30 October 1997, where it is preserved in running condition. The final total of all Comets built at Hatfield and Broughton was seventy-six aircraft, including the two Nimrod prototypes.

13

DH 121 Trident and DH 125 Business Jet

The Trident and DH 125 were the last aircraft to be designed under the de Havilland name, with all Tridents built at Hatfield, and although DH 125s were built at Broughton, all initial design, flight development, training, sales, and customer support were based at Hatfield.

The Trident evolved from a BEA requirement for a short-range airliner issued in July 1956. It called for a jet airliner with more than two engines, preferably located in the rear to reduce cabin noise and accommodation for 80 to 100 passengers in tourist class, with a range of 1,000 miles and a gross weight of 120,000 lb. Despite competitive designs from Bristol and Avro, BEA favoured the de Havilland design, particularly with the company's Comet jet airliner experience. Under pressure from the government to share the overall resource of the project, de Havilland rejuvenated Airco from the First World War, with Hunting and Fairey, to design, develop and manufacture the DH 121, with de Havilland having the majority of 67.5 per cent, Hunting 22.5 per cent, and Fairey 10 per cent. By this time, the project had become a 111-seater with a maximum take-off weight of 123,000 lb and a range of 2,000 miles; it was powered by three 13,500-lb thrust Rolls-Royce Medway bypass jet engines. A market for about 500 was estimated.

After some eighteen months of project design, in May 1959, BEA made radical changes to the specification in the light of projected passenger estimates, which were reduced by over 10 per cent. The airline demanded a much smaller aircraft with an all-up weight of 100,000 lb, accommodation for eighty passengers, but still flying as fast as the original DH 121. With only one launch customer for the new airliner, who was prepared to pay for the redesign, Airco reluctantly scaled down the project and selected three

The original DH 121 Rolls-Royce Medway project for BEA. (*DH Photo*)

9,850-lb thrust Rolls-Royce Spey bypass jets, the smaller aircraft having 40 per cent less thrust, half the range, and 20 per cent less passenger capacity.

With the newly designed Spey engines, any future development prospects were much reduced, the aircraft being produced to the specific BEA route network, rather than broader global requirements. This allowed Boeing to design their 727 to a much more acceptable standard, which was sold in large numbers, leaving the DH 121 with less market appeal. Within three years of requesting the downsizing of the DH 121, BEA executives realised the error in their passenger predictions, making the original proposals ideal for their needs, but too late to revert to the earlier development, allowing the Boeing 727 access to global markets without major competition.

A contract was signed for twenty-four aircraft on 12 August 1959 for delivery of all DH 121s by September 1965; owing to its three engines and triplicated systems, it was named Trident in August 1960. Its triplex control system was to be capable of autoflare initially, followed by full automatic landing by 1970.

In the late 1950s, government policy was mergers within the aerospace industry, and de Havilland believed there was room for Airco to be a third grouping in addition to Hawker Siddeley Aviation (HSA) and British Aircraft Corporation (BAC); however, this was rejected by the Minister of Aviation. The Board of de Havilland therefore opened negotiations with HSA, and an agreement was made to merge the two companies on 17 December 1959, leaving the three members of Airco in different groupings—Hunting with BAC and Fairey with Westland, the latter two companies remaining as sub-contractors in the short term.

The main assembly line was set up in the Hatfield erecting shop where Comets had been built, and as before, the Tridents were built backwards to give clearance for the high tailplane in a 'high bay' at the end. Overall construction of the Trident was similar to the earlier Comet 4s with some nose and fuselage sections produced by HSA companies. The first Trident was set up in jigs in the high bay with the assembly points lined up with optical targets, which today would by automatic laser alignment. Redux bonding was used throughout on both wing and fuselage skins to maintain lighter weight, and the fuselage/wing centre section was integral.

The three Spey engines were located in the tail, with two in pods on the fuselage sides and one at the base of the tail with air fed down an 'S' bend intake from above the cabin ahead of the 'T' tail. With the benefit of automated systems, the flight deck crew consisted of three pilots; weather radar was fitted in the nose. The Trident 1 wing featured a droop leading edge for improved low-speed handling, which on later versions became leading edge slats. To save space, the twin nose wheel undercarriage was offset to port and retracted sideways, while the main undercarriage consisted of four wheels on one axle, twisted through 90 degrees when retracting into fuselage fairings.

The almost-complete first Trident G-ARPA was rolled off the production line at Hatfield on 4 August 1961 fitted with two ground running Speys, one in the port pod and the other in the central position. A considerable amount of flight test instrumentation was fitted in the cabin followed by resonance testing. Taxi tests were carried out to check steering and brake effectiveness, with some adjustments to the undercarriage. By mid-December, flight rated engines were fitted, and although it was cleared for flight on 21 December, the maiden flight was delayed due to heavy snowfall. Following three test 'hops' along the Hatfield runway on 8 January, John Cunningham took the aircraft up on its first flight on 9 January 1962, landing back after one hour and twenty minutes. Five Tridents were allocated to the flight development programme, with G-ARPA being used for low and high-speed handling, including stalling.

G-ARPB was allocated to systems development, including in particular automatic landing. G-ARPC was used for performance measurements with production standard engines and certificate of airworthiness flying. G-ARPD was used for the development of the wing leading edge slats for the improved Trident 1E, and G-ARPE was allocated to BEA for acceptance and route proving flights. The Hatfield team of test pilots was assisted by senior BEA captains to provide training and familiarity with the aircraft. G-ARPB was also used for hot weather trials at Madrid Torrejon, Khartoum, Cairo, and Djibouti.

The first Trident 1 G-ARPA rolled out for the first time at Hatfield on 4 August 1961, without its starboard Spey turbo jet engine. A BEA Comet 4B is in the background on the north apron. (*HSA Photo*)

John Cunningham made the maiden flight of the Trident 1 G-ARPA on 9 January 1962. (*HSA Photo*)

Trident 1 G-ARPB on loan from BEA was the main aircraft used for autoland development, the project pilot being Jimmy Phillips. He made the first autoland at RAE Bedford on 3 March 1964, with the trials continuing until January 1967. On a demonstration for the press on 3 June 1965, Jimmy Phillips and Captain Eric Poole of BEA made nine fully automatic approaches at Gatwick; a week later, G-ARPR made a fully automatic flared touchdown at Paris with passengers.

By this time, G-ARPB had already made over 600 proving flights for autoflare and autoland, and on 4 November 1965, the Trident made the first fully automatic landing at Heathrow when the airport was closed to all other traffic due to fog. The challenge was to find the way from the runway to a terminal. The overall autoland development programme involved some 2,000 landings, and by May 1967, BEA had begun to use autoland in regular operations, with clearance to Cat 2 (150 feet decision height and 500 m runway visual range (RVR)) in February 1969, leading to Cat 3A limits of 200-m RVR. Trident 2E G-AVFA was flown for 170 hours on autoland development from Hatfield, to establish Cat 3A clearance and extend the clearance for both Trident 1s and 2s to Cat 3B limits of 50-m RVR.

When flying around Europe with BEA, it was known that passengers would arrive at their expected destination in all weathers, whereas international long-haul flights in winter could be diverted anywhere there was a safe haven. The cost of developing automatic landing in all weathers was more than justified by avoiding cancelling or diverting flights in adverse weather conditions. Autoland is now used in all modern airliners.

To achieve a full transport category certificate of airworthiness, there had to be a clear warning of an impending stall, with the nose pitched down strongly should the pilot hold back too long. With a high 'T' tail, there was a tendency for the aircraft to enter a deep or stable stall, where the tail was blanketed by the wing, also stopping air entering the engine intakes. Initially, a warning was given by a stick shaker, followed by a stick pusher, with a vane on either side of the cockpit sensing the break-down of airflow. During high-speed trials, G-ARPA achieved Mach 0.96 in a shallow dive from 30,000 to 25,000 feet, equivalent to a speed of 652 and 667 mph, with a level speed of Mach 0.9 or 627 mph, making the Trident the fastest airliner in service at the time.

By June 1963, total flying time for the five Tridents was close to 1,000 hours, with just 200 hours to go on route proving. With the test programme close to completion G-ARPA, 'C, 'D, and 'E were flown to Hawker Siddeley at Bitteswell for bringing up to full production standard, while G-ARPB was leased back to HSA for three and a half years of intensive autoland trials. The Trident certificate of airworthiness was awarded on 18

Comet 2E (formerly G-AMXK with Smiths Instruments, and later XV144 with the BLEU at RAE Bedford) used for Trident autoland development. (*Author's collection*)

Comet 3B XP915 ex-G-ANLO at Hatfield before delivery to BLEU at RAE Bedford for Trident autoland development. (*Author's collection*)

February 1964, with a formal handover on 28 February, allowing *ad hoc* services to commence on 11 March after some 2,300 flight development hours, with full services from 1 April from Heathrow to Zurich. The final Trident 1 G-ARPZ was delivered to BEA on 1 July 1966 with Tridents flying through the European networks, replacing Vickers Viscounts.

On a sunny 3 June 1966 afternoon, Trident 1 G-ARPY was taken up for its routine first production test flight. In command was Peter Barlow, who had previously been a Sea Vixen test pilot, but had taken part in the Trident programme, flying 1,600 hours and participated in 2,195 stalls, including 750 as pilot in command. The author's task was to find the remainder of the crew, which was particularly demanding that Friday afternoon. Edgar Brackstone-Brown (Brax), the chief flight engineer, was on board to look after the systems and advised when the aircraft was ready for flight. Charles Paterson was on board to check the radios and communication equipment, but we were still looking for a co-pilot. I looked out of my office window in the control tower and the Cirrus Moth G-EBLV kept in flying condition by the company taxied in after a short familiarisation flight by George Errington. George had been chief test pilot at Christchurch for the Ambassador flight development programme, and while still living on the south coast, he worked at Hatfield on customer liaison and enjoyed keeping current with flying. I called down and asked him if he was able to help crew this first test, and he agreed with great enthusiasm, collecting his headset and going out to the aircraft on the compass base. The Trident taxied past the control tower and departed at 4.52 p.m.

The flight test schedule took the aircraft out over East Anglia and up the east coast where there was very little conflicting traffic and good telemetry reception at Hatfield. At around 6.30 p.m., three stall approaches were made with the recovery systems operative to ensure they were functioning, and then a fourth with them switched off as required in the flight test schedule, but Peter Barlow delayed carrying out full stall recovery, the aircraft entering a deep stall. By this time, I was at home near the aerodrome, when I received a call from Len Gaskins in air traffic to say he had received a call from 'PY about thirty minutes before when Peter Barlow said 'am in a deep stall—standby'. Len had not realised the significance of the message, and I had to tell him we had lost an aircraft. The Trident impacted the ground with little forward movement near Coltishall in Norfolk killing the four crew members, and messages soon began to come through from the RAF and local rescue services.

While on the sad subject of flight crew losses when testing aircraft, even during the 1960s, during the author's time as PA to John Cunningham, there was loss from Hawarden. Test pilot Alan Brandon and flight test

Eight Trident 1s for BEA being built backwards in the erecting shop at Hatfield. (*HSA Photo*)

Six BEA Trident 1s in the flight test hangar during the flight development programme. (*HSA Photo*)

Trident 1 G-ARPY on pressure test, prior to first production test flight on 3 June 1966, when it was lost in a deep stall. (*Author's collection*)

observer Tony Chalke were responsible for production testing the many aircraft built in the Broughton factory. Their workday could be anything from a Chipmunk to an overhauled RAF Blackburn Beverley transport, with a HS 125 and other types in between. They were tasked with flight testing Austrian Air Force Vampire Trainer 5C-YA following its overhaul at Broughton. After take-off on 18 April 1966, they climbed away, but during the sortie there was total electrical failure with loss of airspeed information, the canopy was jettisoned, and the aircraft hit high ground near Llangollen in a snowstorm. Tony Chalke's body was found in the wreckage, and although Alan had ejected moments before impact, his parachute did not have time to open properly and his body was found nearby, where he had died of exposure.

There was one other aircraft loss at Hatfield while I was working with John Cunningham, but fortunately, it was not fatal. George Aird was coming into land in Lightning F.1a XG332 on 13 September 1962, when a fire started during finals to land, causing a tailplane control failure, pitching the aircraft violently nose up. George was able to eject before the aircraft crashed, but his parachute did not have time to open at such low altitude, and he fell on greenhouses on the aerodrome boundary, which fortunately broke his fall into a mass of tomatoes. He suffered two broken legs and other injuries but was flying again within six months, although he had lost an inch or two in height.

These were dedicated, highly skilled, and professional people who paid the ultimate price in peacetime to make aviation safer for future generations. John Hanslip, Ken Rouse, Peter Barlow, George Errington, Brax, Charles Paterson, Alan Brandon, and Tony Chalke were all known to the author and fulfilled their flying duties, despite the risks that were not apparent, but which caught them out.

The first Trident development was the export Trident 1E with improved airfield performance and extended wingspan by 5 feet plus the drooped leading-edge slats as developed on G-ARPD. Power came from 11,400-lb thrust Spey 511s, with an additional fuel capacity and increased all-up weight. The auxiliary power unit (APU) was relocated from the aircraft underside to a tail fairing, which was also retrofitted to the BEA aircraft. The first of three Trident 1Es (G-ASWU/9K-ACF) for Kuwait Airways flew on 2 November 1964 and was used for certification trials of the new variant. To supply an anticipated Middle Eastern market, fifteen airframes were laid down on the production line, but in the event, only three more were ordered by Iraqi Airways and four by Pakistan International Airways (PIA), one of which was delivered to the Pakistan Air Force. The sale to PIA proved very significant, as their Tridents were later sold to CAAC of China, resulting in significant additional orders. This left five unsold Trident 1Es on the Hatfield production line which HSA were keen to place in airline service, resulting in an order for all five from Channel Airways on 5 October 1967 for a special adaptation with high-density inclusive tours as Trident 1E-140s. The seating was increased from 115 to 139 passengers, requiring an additional passenger escape exit to be installed over the wing.

The first Channel Trident 1E (G-AVYB) was delivered on 31 May 1968, entering service on 13 June from Stansted, followed by the second and final aircraft a month later. The airline had problems financing the order, with the fleet remaining at two Tridents; the airline ceased operations at the end of 1971. Two of the intended Channel Trident 1E-140s were sold to Newcastle-based BKS, 70 per cent owned by BEA, which were delivered in March and April 1969, the airline name changing in November 1970 to Northeast. When Channel closed down, their two Tridents were passed to Northeast, which was fully merged with BEA in March 1976. The remaining Trident 1E on the production line was sold to Air Ceylon, leaving Hatfield on 19 July 1969, remaining in service until July 1978, when it was withdrawn for ground instruction training.

A longer-range development, the Trident 2E with a range capability of London to Beirut non-stop was ordered by BEA on 5 August 1965 for fifteen aircraft with options on a further ten. The gross weight was increased over the 1C by 8,500 lb to 143,500 lb with more powerful 11,930-lb thrust Spey 25 engines with additional 350-gallon fuel tank in the tail. Drag was reduced by fitting Kuchemann wingtips, the first Trident

PIA Trident 1E AP-ATL which was later sold to CAAC of China, resulting in major Trident orders. In the background on the left is the Engine Company flight test hangar and in the middle is the Blue Streak test tower, beyond the Propeller flight test hangars. (*Author's collection*)

Channel Airways Trident 1E-130 G-AVYE on the north apron with No. 1 engine being changed 27 March 1968, with detail shops behind and white restaurant in background. (*Author's collection*)

2E G-AVFA making its maiden flight from Hatfield on 27 July 1967 with John Cunningham in command. In addition to hot and high trials, this aircraft reached Mach 0.97, and despite being very close to Mach 1, there were no handling problems. G-AVFA replaced G-ARPB on autoland trials, eventually being delivered to BEA on 2 December 1969. Trident 2Es entered service with BEA on an *ad hoc* basis, starting with G-AVFD on 17 April 1968 from London to Milan, with regular services commencing on 1 June; all the aircraft were delivered to BEA with full autoland capability. Cyprus Airways ordered two Trident 2Es in March 1969, the first released by BEA 5B-DAA being delivered on 18 September 1969; later, the airline added the two former Kuwait 1Es. In July 1974, Cyprus Airways ceased operations when Nicosia Airport was put out of action by the Turkish attack, two of the Tridents being destroyed and two others damaged but recovered by BEA three years later.

A major operator of Trident 2Es was CAAC of China. PIA had operated their Trident 1Es to Beijing, and as already mentioned sold on their aircraft to China when they withdrew them from service in June 1970. After lengthy negotiations by the HSA sales team, CAAC ordered an initial batch of six Trident 2Es in August 1971, followed by six more a year later, with options on six more. These options were taken up three months later, in addition to a contract for two Trident Super 3Bs. On 19 November 1972, the first Trident 2E departed Hatfield on delivery to China, and a final order was placed for a further fifteen Trident 2Es in December 1973. The 117th and last Trident completed left Hatfield on 28 June 1978, having kept the production line busy for five years. The Chinese Tridents had a crew of five—two pilots, a flight engineer, a navigator, and radio officer; also, autoland was not fitted. The aircraft remained in service until 1991.

The ultimate development was the stretched Trident 3B with 135 seats to be used on BEA short-range, high-density routes such as London to Manchester, Paris, and Amsterdam. BEA was not enthusiastic about the Trident 3, regarding it as too small, too late, and too expensive. Despite wanting to buy British, BEA looked at a mixed fleet of Boeing 727-200s and 737-200s, but the Labour Government rejected the proposal and instructed the airline to look at domestically produced aircraft. Competition from BAC resulted in development costs that were too high, making the Trident 3B the logical answer as it could carry 60 per cent more payload than the Trident 1, with only 20 per cent increase in operating weight over 25 per cent increased range. The Trident fleet was complimented by a larger version of the BAC 111.

BEA accepted that it had to order the Trident 3B but demanded compensation from the government, signing a contract for twenty-six

John Cunningham made the first flight of Trident 2 G-AVFA on 27 July 1967, his birthday. (*Author's collection*)

CAAC Trident 2 G-AZFY/250, 9 November 1973. (*Author's collection*)

HS 132 project based on the Trident 3 powered by a pair of large fan engines, May 1975. (*HSA Photo*)

Trident 3Bs worth £83 million, the largest ever airliner order for the British aircraft industry. The Trident Three had the fuselage lengthened by 8 feet 5 inches forward of the wing centre section, and 8 feet aft, making room for 146 passengers in a mixed-class layout, or up to 180 all in economy. Aerodynamic changes were limited to wing incidence increased by 2 degrees to give rear fuselage ground clearance for take-off, an increase in span of wing flaps, and other minor improvements. Power was from three 11,960-lb thrust Speys, assisted by a tail-mounted Rolls-Royce RB162 lift engine developing 5,230-lb thrust to boost take-off and initial climb; the APU was relocated to the top of the centre engine intake. The booster engine reduced the take-off run by 1,500 feet, despite a 6,500-lb increase in aircraft weight; however, due to the high noise level, the power was cut with the booster as the airport boundary was crossed.

The first Trident 3B was rolled out on 17 November 1969. Following ground tests, John Cunningham and his team took it off from Hatfield on its maiden flight on 11 December with a mock-up booster engine fitted. The first boosted take-off was from RAE Bedford on 26 March 1970, with G-AWYZ being allocated to general handling, high-speed trials, booster engine performance and autoland evaluation. The second aircraft G-AWZA was handed over the BEA for crew training in December 1970 with the certificate of airworthiness awarded on 8 February 1971 ready

Rolls-Royce booster engine at the base of the rudder on Trident 3 G-AWYZ at Hatfield, 19 February 1970. (*Author's collection*)

to enter service on 11 March, flying from London to Madrid. As the new development became established in service, BEA expressed a high level of satisfaction, with departure reliability better than 96 per cent. Tridents became the backbone of BEA operations with a total of sixty-four new aircraft, and six second-hand examples.

BEA and BOAC merged in 1974 to become British Airways (BA), with some of the Tridents being allocated to a shuttle operation commencing with the London–Glasgow Shuttle from 12 January 1975, providing an hourly standby service on weekdays and two hours at weekends. As the shuttle was expanded to include Edinburgh, Manchester, and Belfast, Trident Threes were also added, the regularity being guaranteed with the use of autoland in all weathers.

As already mentioned, CAAC ordered two 152-seat Trident Super 3Bs with an increased all-up weight and additional fuel capacity increasing range by 25 per cent. The pair were delivered to China—B-268 on 22 August and B-270 on 26 September 1975.

With the introduction of new aircraft engine noise regulations by the end of 1985, it was impossible for the Tridents to comply, and they were gradually withdrawn and either scrapped or allocated for crash rescue training around major British airports. The final commercial BA flights were a pair of enthusiast services into Heathrow on 31 December 1985, while operations in China continued until well into the 1990s.

Hatfield aerodrome in August 1977 with the flight test hangar and the Manor Road site including the large purpose-built Engine Company hangar. (*HSA Photo*)

CAAC Trident Super 3 and 2 in the high bay of the erecting shop, 11 March 1975.

First CAAC Trident Super 3 made its maiden flight from Hatfield by John Cunningham on 9 July 1975. (*HSA Photo*)

DH 125 Business Jet

The first two prototype DH 125s were built at Broughton but assembled at Hatfield, where the design engineering team could keep a check on progress. Initial business jet studies had started in 1956–57 based on de Havilland jet airliner experience. The basic Dove concept with two pilots and cabin for six passengers appeared an ideal configuration, with a jet cruising speed of around 500 mph and longer range. North America represented the largest potential market for business jets, resulting in a cruise range from coast to coast in the USA with one stop. The cabin would need to be with stand-up headroom and fitted with a separate toilet. The twin rear-mounted jet engine aircraft had an estimated initial market of 200, but to be competitive, it had to be less expensive and faster than the American equivalent. Although the de Havilland Board rejected the programme, the cancellation of Blue Streak made a large number of skilled engineers without work, and it was Sir Geoffrey de Havilland who suggested the go-ahead of the business jet to provide employment for these people.

For simplicity, the one-piece wing passed under the fuselage, giving uninterrupted cabin floor space. The light and inexpensive structure provided ample fuel capacity in integral fuel tanks, while the double-slotted flaps allowed operations from rough strips 4,500 feet long. The modest cruising speed of 500 mph resulted in the flying controls being manual, saving weight and cost. The engines selected were Bristol Siddeley Viper 520s, which had flown around 200,000 hours in RAF Jet Provost trainers and developed 2,580-lb thrust. Board approval was given on 10 March 1961 for full engineering development to commence, with an initial production batch of thirty aircraft, twenty of which would be delivered to the RAF as navigation trainers.

The first 125 G-ARYA were transported to Hatfield by road, leaving Broughton in March 1962 and after assembly and painting was flown for the first time by project test pilot Chris Capper and flight development engineer John Rye on 13 August 1962, followed by the second aircraft on 12 December the same year. This started an intensive flight development programme with resources shared with the Trident and Sea Vixen FAW.2 flight testing—a major undertaking that overall was achieved on time and cost.

The DH 125 used de Havilland experience to produce an airliner in miniature, with a rugged structure; the third aircraft (G-ARYC) was the first built to production standard with the fuselage lengthened by 12 inches, allowing the main inward opening door to open, and airstairs lowered from the sill. This aircraft was the first to be flown from Hawarden on 12 February 1963 and was delivered on 24 July to Bristol Siddeley Engines at Filton, for Viper engine development and civil certification. Meanwhile, the flight development programme continued from Hatfield with the certificate of airworthiness being achieved on 28 July 1964 after flying over 2,200 hours total.

In addition to the two development prototypes, eight Series 1s were produced before production was divided into two streams—1A for the North American market and Series 1B for the rest of the world. The Series 1As were delivered 'green' across the North Atlantic followed by equipping, furnishing, and painting at Canadian and USA completion centres, the first aircraft for America being delivered in September 1964. The first 1B was delivered to the Australian DCA and the new versions benefitted from 3,120-lb thrust Viper 521s, an increase in gross weight and the range increased by 120 miles.

The 125s Series 2s were Dominie navigation trainers for the RAF, production of which was spread out over a period of time to allow customer deliveries of the improved Series 1As and 1Bs. The contract was placed in April 1964 with service entry in December 1965 to 1 ANS at Stradishall. The Dominie cabin had accommodation for two pupils and an instructor, the navigators being trained mainly for the V-Bomber force. Further examples served with the College of Air Warfare (CAW) at Manby and RAF College at Cranwell until all non-pilot aircrew training was allocated to 6 FTS at Finningley. Dominies were finally retired prematurely on 20 January 2011 as a result of Conservative Government Strategic Defence Review in 2010.

First prototype DH 125 G-ARYA on the north apron at Hatfield after its first flight by Chris Capper and John Rye on 13 August 1962. (*Author's collection*)

The second prototype DH 125 G-ARYB was also assembled at Hatfield, where it made its first flight departing on 12 December 1962. (*HSA Photo*)

First production DH 125 G-ARYC completed at Broughton and delivered to Bristol Siddeley for Viper engine development, later used by Rolls-Royce for Viper 600 development, at Hatfield on 4 November 1970. (*Author's collection*)

The first four DH 125s ready for the day's development flying in front of the old flying school on 28 May 1963. (*HSA Photo*)

DH 125s G-ARYC leading with HB-VAG for Chartag, G-ARYB and G-ASEC flying over the edge of Hatfield aerodrome with Hatfield Polytechnic in the background, May 1964. (*HSA Photo*)

DH 125 No. 8 G-ASSI on return to Hatfield on 17 November following its North American tour, with twenty-two sales silhouettes on the nose. (*Author's collection*)

A photo of opportunity: DH 125 HB-VAG for Chartag in formation with Trident 1 G-ARPB. (*Author's collection*)

HS 125 No. 9 XW930 was used by RAE Bedford for noise structural shielding research. (*Author's collection*)

The Series 3 was introduced from the end of 1966 with power from 3,360-lb thrust Viper 522 engines, improved air conditioning and pressurisation, and the fitting of an APU to provide better autonomy at underequipped airfields. The first aircraft to this standard were a pair to Qantas for pilot crew training; fuel capacity was increased in the 3B/RA by fitting a 112-gallon fuel tank in a fairing under the rear fuselage.

With sales going well, to maintain the momentum among the growing global competition, the Series 400 was created, making improvements to the airframe by reducing drag, but maintaining the same Vipers, as by this time, Bristol Siddeley was part of Rolls-Royce, who at the time were not offering any Viper improvements. The entry door was reduced in width to 27 inches and hinged downwards to create integral airstairs. Despite concerns, the improvements were not enough; there were fifty orders in 1968 and another forty-four in 1969, the first Series 400 being delivered across the Atlantic in September 1968, this version remaining in production until July 1973. After just over nine years from the first flight, the 250th sale was celebrated at Hatfield on 15 September 1971; nine invited customer aircraft were lined up on the grass, facing four company 125s and twenty-two national flags, representing the countries where the 125 had been sold.

Ten customer HS 125s lined up on the grass at Hatfield on 15 September 1971 to celebrate the 250th sale of the business jet in twenty-two countries. (*Author's collection*)

Development costs were always achieved on a low budget for the HS 125 to maintain a competitive price in the marketplace. With support from Rolls-Royce in the development of the increased-power Viper 600, the first example ran in August 1966 with a take-off rating of 3,750-lb thrust. Considerations were given to fitting the new engine to the Series 400 airframe as the Series 500, but there were few benefits. However, it was decided to increase the fuselage length by 24 inches ahead of the wing incorporating an additional window, balancing it out with a taller fin. The cabin was reconfigured, and other changes included improved avionics. The new Viper 602 required noise suppression to allow the engine to meet noise regulations in the 1974–76 timeframe. Fuel capacity was increased by a 50-gallon tank in the dorsal fin, allowing a full payload of six passengers and baggage over a range of 1,570 nautical miles.

Two Series 400 airframes were allocated on the Broughton production line for conversion to Series 600 prototypes, with the first prototype (G-AYBH) flying unpainted on 21 January 1971 to Hatfield for flight development. The second aircraft was ready a few days later, but with the bankruptcy of Rolls-Royce due to problems with the RB.211 fan jets for the Lockheed TriStar, no further Vipers could be supplied until new contracts had been agreed. The second aircraft (G-AZHS) was finally flown to Hatfield on 25 November 1971. Although there was a global economic depression at the time, the HSA Board approved an initial production batch of thirty-eight, with the first example delivered to the USA in May 1972 for completion as a North American demonstrator. The first 125-600B was sold to Green Shield Stamps and two more were added to RAF 32 Squadron's fleet, based at Northolt. Although the 125-600 was a significant step in the HS 125 programme, the aircraft lacked significant range, and the Viper was at the end of its development life, particularly with regards to noise regulations. Only seventy-two 125-600s were built with the last delivered in November 1976.

The HS 125 was the only business jet not powered by the quieter and more fuel-efficient turbofan engines, and the 1973 oil crisis caused fuel to rise by a factor of ten over two years, making the 125 uncompetitive. The development of smaller turbofan engines gave much-reduced noise and a 60 per cent increase in range for a lighter weight. The Hatfield design team had been studying available turbofan engines since 1972–73, the most practical being the Garrett TFE731, which gave business jets non-stop coast-to-coast range in the USA. The decision to go ahead with this engine was made in mid-1975 but not revealed publicly until 12 May 1976 to avoid depressing further the already poor 125-600 sales prospects. The new version was designated the 125 Series 700, and apart from the adaptation of the engine mounts,

HS 125-600 G-AZHS taking off from Hatfield in June 1970 over the erecting shop and technical services (previously the experimental department). (*HSA Photo*)

changes to the airframe were minimal and a new Collins flight control system was installed.

The original Series 600B demonstrator (G-AZHS) was returned to the Broughton factory to be converted to the Series 700 prototype. It was rolled out on 21 June with a striking new colour scheme and new registration—G-BFAN; it was flown for the first time on 28 June 1976 by Mike Goodfellow. It was soon confirmed that noise levels were much reduced and fuel economy was at least as good as expected, with certification obtained in Britain and the USA in May 1977. The new aircraft had a range increase of 1,000 miles without any increase in fuel capacity. In addition to flight checking of upper airways, 125-700s were adopted for a number of special duties, including maritime surveillance and photo survey. The first production 125-700 (G-BEDZ) flew on 8 November 1976 with the range increased ultimately to 2,600 miles. The 400th 125 sale was celebrated at Broughton on 20 April 1978 with a line-up of thirteen invited customer aircraft, together with the first production 125-700. This version proved to be the most successful with 215 aircraft sold until 1983. In April 1977, Hawker Siddeley Aviation became part of the nationalised British Aerospace, which was privatised in 1981, the type becoming known as the BAe 125.

Following the 125-700's success, TFE731 fan engines were also offered as retrofits on all apart from the Series 1, 1A, and 1Bs; a total of sixty-five aircraft were converted, giving 70 per cent added range and improved airfield performance.

HS 125-700 final assembly at Broughton on 5 May 1977 with A300 wing jigs and equipping in the background. (*HS Photo*)

The 400th HS 125 sale was celebrated at Broughton on 20 April 1978 with thirteen customer aircraft present. (*Author's collection*)

In April 1981, the BAe Board sanctioned the design go-ahead for the Series 800 featuring major aerodynamic improvements with the first aircraft flying from Hawarden on 26 May 1983. The most obvious change was a curved flight deck windscreen; other improvements included a redesigned rear fuselage and tail, increased span outer wings, a new EFIS flight deck, and uprated engines. The first aircraft (G-BKTF) was allocated to the Hatfield flight development programme. The second aircraft (G-DCCC) flew on 24 June and was allocated to systems testing and performance evaluation. The third aircraft was the first fitted with EFIS, and following 840 hours flight testing, certification was awarded in May 1984.

The largest and final major variant of the 125 was designated BAe 1000; it had transatlantic range and a longer cabin with added seats and increased baggage capacity, the overall range being 3,500 miles. Power came from 5,236-lb thrust Pratt & Whitney PW305 with even better fuel efficiency. The enlarged cabin and increased fuel capacity were achieved by a complete redesign of the fuselage adding 18 inches ahead of the wing, and 15 inches aft. Apart from local strengthening, the wing design changed little and all systems were modernised. The new cabin was certificated to accommodate up to fifteen passengers with a full galley. The first 1000 G-EXLR flew from Hawarden on 16 June 1990, followed by G-OPFC in honour of Peter Cedarvall, the 125's chief designer for some twenty years, on 26 November, then G-ELRA on 23 February 1991. CAA certification was achieved on 19 October 1991, with FAA approval ten days later, by which time development flying had been transferred to Woodford near Manchester.

In 1989, BAe divided the Civil Aircraft Division into three parts with the 125 becoming the responsibility of Hatfield-based Corporate Jets, and the company put up for sale. With further reorganisation, Corporate Jets became a subsidiary of BAe Inc at Dulles with a sale to Raytheon on 1 June 1993. The new company became Raytheon Corporate Jets as part of Beechcraft, with production of the main airframe parts continuing at Broughton and shipped to the USA for assembly and completion. At the 2012 NBAA business aircraft show in Florida, Beechcraft announced on 29 October that in order to emerge from bankruptcy protection, all production and development of business jets including the Hawker 800 and 1000 would cease, as well as a major programme of new business jets in the development and planning stage. A total of 1,852 125s of all variants were built and many are still in global operation in a variety of roles.

First production BAe 125-800 (G-BKTF) during flight development at Hatfield 1 July 1983. (*Author's collection*)

BAe 125-800 development aircraft G-BKUW was first flown from Hawarden by Mike Goodfellow on 26 May 1983, then joined the flight development programme at Hatfield. (*BAe Photo*)

14

Airbus Wing:
Centre of Excellence

In June 1965, aerospace industry discussions began between Britain and France on future airliner designs leading to co-operation on the design, development, and production of what was referred to as the European Airbus (a large capacity short–medium range transport for service entry from the mid-1970s). At about the same time, an Airbus study group was formed in Germany, and in January 1966, initial negotiations were held between government representatives of the three countries, with the first official agreement for Airbus joint development reached in September 1966.

On 15 October, a basic specification was submitted for official approval of a projected A300; it was the basis for a formal presentation to airlines in March 1967. On 26 September 1967, the three governments gave the Airbus consortium authority to continue design studies and project definition. This agreement nominated Hawker Siddeley Aviation at Hatfield, Sud Aviation (later Aerospatiale) and Deutsche Airbus as the airframe partner developers, together with Rolls-Royce, SNECMA, and MAN-Turbo (now MTU) as the engine partners. Leadership of the airframe was with Aerospatiale and engines with Rolls-Royce.

It was agreed by the governments that joint approval would be given for production provided seventy-five sales were achieved, including the national airlines from each of the three countries. Under the terms of the agreement, Britain and France were each to have 37.5 per cent of work share on the project and Germany the remaining 25 per cent.

In December 1968, the British and French partners proposed a reduced size configuration, as the original was believed to be too large, the new 250 seat airliner being designated the A300B. The reduced size resulted in new engines not needing to be developed, as existing Rolls-Royce RB 211, Pratt & Whitney JT9D, and General Electric CF6 turbofans were ideally suited to the project. As insufficient sales had been received, including no interest by British Airways, the British Government withdrew on 10 April 1969, leaving Hawker Siddeley Aviation without support.

A new agreement was reached between France and Germany on 29 May 1969, with Germany prepared to contribute 50 per cent of the project costs if France was prepared to do the same. In addition, Hawker Siddeley decided that the company should remain with the project as a favoured sub-contractor, with total design responsibility for developing and manufacturing A300B wings in collaboration with Fokker-VFW, who were building the wing moving control surfaces under an agreement with the Dutch Government. Airbus Industrie was formally created on 18 December 1970, and in 1971, CASA of Spain became a third full partner with 4.2 per cent share, the other two members reducing their share to 47.9 per cent each. In 1979, British Aerospace joined the consortium by acquiring a 20 per cent share in Airbus Industrie with France and Germany reducing their shares to 37.9 per cent each.

The A300B was a single-deck, twin-turbofan airliner with twin aisles and seating for up to 261 passengers, flown by a crew of two. The initial A300B1 was powered by two 49,000-lb thrust General Electric CF6-50A engines installed in pods identical with the wing-mounted engines on the McDonnell Douglas DC-10 airliner.

Final assembly was set up at Toulouse Blagnac Airport, the many major assemblies being transported from all over Europe to the final assembly line, the wings being manufactured, equipped and assembled at Broughton, where Airbus wing production continues today. Wing design was centred at Hatfield, the aerodynamics being developed from Trident experience featuring a super-critical wing section giving a highly economic performance, and advanced aerodynamically efficient flying control surfaces. Hatfield was also where CAD/CAM (Computer Aided Design/Computer Aided Machining) was used to router machine the rolled aluminium wing skins. The skins were too large to clamp down mechanically, so they were laid on a vacuum machine bed with milling machine on tracks down each side. The main undercarriage rib 5 forged mounting for the pivot point was also machined in the Technical Services Department, previously known as Experimental Department. The finished skins and rib 5 forgings were then delivered to Broughton for assembly in the vertical jigs where they could be lifted out on completion by a pair of the overhead cranes running along roof-mounted tracks.

To transport the wings and other main assemblies from around Europe, a fleet of four Boeing 377 Stratofreighter-derived Super Guppies aircraft were acquired by Airbus. With the airfield at Hawarden being too short for Super Guppy operations, a pair of wings were mounted on a special stand and taken by road to Manchester Airport, where they were loaded and flown to Bremen for fitting the moveable control surfaces. From there, wings were flown singly to Toulouse, as a pair with the control surfaces would not fit in a Super Guppy. As a result, manufacturers were able to supply assemblies fully fitted with systems to the final assembly at Toulouse in a flight time of no more than two hours. This made the A300B the first airliner to be produced using 'just-in-time' assembly techniques.

The wings were cantilever mid-fuselage-mounted with a sweepback of 28 degrees at quarter chord with an overall span of 147 feet 1.25 inches—all dimensions being imperial and not metric as the world's airlines were used to operating aircraft from Britain and America. The primary wing structure was a two-spar box type built with high strength aluminium alloy, with a third spar along the wider inboard section. Each wing had three section leading-edge slats and three trailing edge-mounted Fowler-type double-slotted flaps. There were all-speed ailerons between the inboard and outboard flaps, and a low-speed aileron at each wingtip outboard the flaps. Lift dump for landing was by the use of spoilers, with airbrakes inboard on each wing.

Construction commenced of the first A300B1 prototype at Toulouse in September 1969 and made its first flight on 28 October 1972; the second aircraft flew on 5 February 1973. They were later followed by two of the longer A300B2 development aircraft. After 1,580 flying hours, type certification was achieved on 23 May 1974, with the first production aircraft entering service with Air France, making the first commercial flight on 20 May 1974 from Paris to London and return.

Following the A300B in development was the shorter A310; then the single-aisle A320 family, including the shorter A319 and stretched A321; A330 twin-engined long-range airliner replacing the A300B, and complemented by the four-engined A340 long-range airliner; the A380 long-range large-capacity twin deck airliner; and the recently developed A350 airliner, which uses composites in its construction. The A320 family is now benefiting from a new engine update, giving greater economy and range for reduced noise; it was designated A320neo. Similar improvements are being made to the A330neo, while the A340 is coming out of service due to poor competitive economics. The A380 has a limited customer base, but it continues in reduced production, mainly for Emirates, in the anticipation of growing future global markets. Airbus has grown significantly providing equal competition to Boeing of the USA, to the overall benefit of worldwide air travel.

A complex NC machining task at Hatfield was the Airbus main undercarriage pinion Rib 5 forging with wing skin NC machining in the background. (*BAe Photo*)

The unconventional arrival of Super Guppy F-BTGV at Manchester Airport 22 November 1971 to collect the first set of A300B wings. If a nose up attitude was adopted, the aircraft would just float along the runway without touching down. (*Author's collection*)

The first set of A300B wings loaded into the Super Guppy at Manchester Airport on 22 November 1971, ready for delivery to Bremen where the control surfaces were assembled before delivery to the final assembly line at Toulouse. (*Author's collection*)

The first A300B commercial service was with Air France F-BVGA from Paris to London on 20 May 1974. (*Author's collection*)

On the closing of the Hatfield facility and aerodrome, all Airbus wing design was moved to Filton near Bristol, where there was also some aerostructures work supplying Broughton. In April 2006, BAE Systems announced the sale of the company's 20 per cent stake in Airbus Industrie to concentrate on its military business, particularly in the USA, where it was the fifth biggest defence contractor. At the time, there was also a high financial liability with development of the A380 Super Jumbo jet airliner. At this time, BAE Systems employed nearly 13,000 people in the UK, manufacturing wings for the Airbus airliners. There was concern that work may be lost to other partners in the programme. However, in October 2012, BAE Systems approached Airbus partners to rejoin the consortium, but although there was support from the British Government (including investing in launch aid for the new A350 airliner) and enthusiasm from EADS, any agreement was blocked by the German Government. Tom Enders (the Airbus group chief executive) wanted the merger to curb political interference with the company, with each government having a non-voting golden share.

15

BAe 146: Britain's Most Successful Jet Airliner

The concept of the BAe 146 began in the de Havilland Future Projects Department in the late 1950s with 'Dakota replacement' DH 123 twin-turboprop up to forty-passenger airliner project, which evolved into the DH 126 'T' tail airliner. Following the merger with Hawker Siddeley in 1960, the project evolved into the HS 131, later becoming the HS 136 with a similar layout to the Boeing 737, which was powered by a pair of underwing Rolls-Royce Trent turbofans and capable of carrying up to fifty-seven passengers. This layout was abandoned in 1968 and changed to a rear-engined high-tail design. After a comparative evaluation between Hatfield and the Woodford design teams, the two combined to create the HS 144 with rear-mounted Trent engines and a high tailplane. With Rolls-Royce's bankruptcy, the Trent programme was cancelled, leaving the project without power. However, there was a fan engine available from an unexpected source—the American Avco Lycoming ALF 502 developing a modest 6,700-lb thrust, with four engines being required instead of two, resulting in the high-wing BAe 146 airliner.

Having four engines instead of two raised the perception of increased complexity, especially for short-haul operations, which created some resistance from airlines. On a positive note, the four engines gave excellent airfield performance at undeveloped and 'downtown' airports without the complexity and additional weight of high lift wing devices and reverse thrust. The quietness and slow landing speeds were also a benefit to surrounding communities close to airports. Modern turbofan engines are very reliable, requiring minimum maintenance, and having four engines resulted in greater fuel economy due to less overall installed thrust required in the event of an engine failure.

Fourth DH 125 G-ASEC fitted with a stone catching device for ground trials in the HS 136 project, to check for gravel damage to the predicted engine positions. (*Author's collection*)

Market research identified the BAe 146 as a jet-powered replacement for the earlier turboprop Woodford-produced HS 748 and Fokker F-27, offering good economics on short to medium routes. It was vital that high reliability was achieved in the demanding regional air transport market with short sectors and multiple landings and take-offs.

The Hawker Siddeley Board announced the go-ahead of the HS 146 on 29 August 1973, with the government providing launching aid of £46 million to be recovered from a levy on sales; this investment was matched by the company, although there were no orders from airlines at the time. The intention was to offer two versions to the market, the seventy–eighty-eight-seat 146-100 and the eighty-two–102-seat 146-200, with an overall length of 85 feet 10 inches and 93 feet 1 inch respectively, and an identical wingspan of 86 feet 6 inches. Responsibility for design, final assembly, and flight testing would be at Hatfield, with major assemblies built at Hatfield, including the forward fuselage, and other parts from the HSA factories at Woodford and Brough. No allocation was made initially for wing construction, but Woodford would build the wing control surfaces, tail, and rear fuselage, while Brough would build the nose.

Although work on the project progressed well, the oil crisis and high inflation started the worst economic recession since the war. Programme costs rose significantly to some £120 million, and with HSA responsible for any overrun, it would create a liability well beyond the company's financial resources. In addition, it was highly likely that the Labour Government elected to power in February 1974 would nationalise the British aerospace industry. As a result of the combined situation, on 17 September 1974, the workforce was informed the Board believed the project was financially unviable.

Work was halted on 21 October, by which time a full-scale wooden mock-up had been constructed in Technical Services; the government was informed, but redundancy notices were withheld. There were protests and demonstration by the workers at Hatfield and Brough with support from Tony Benn (Minister of Industry) and Helen Hayman (the Labour MP for Hatfield). On 9 December, Tony Benn stated that fifty-fifty funding was no longer practical, but the government wished to maintain a civil airliner capability when the aerospace industry was nationalised. It was agreed to maintain the jigs and tools, drawings, and design capacity to keep options open for a restart of the project, although the Treasury was opposed to supporting the programme financially.

In April 1977, the Government-owned British Aerospace was formed, taking over the aerospace responsibilities of Hawker Siddeley and the British Aircraft Corporation, later adding Scottish Aviation at Prestwick. The unions continued to kept up the pressure with MPs and the BAe Board resulting in an announcement in the Commons on 10 July 1978 by Gerald Kaufman (Minister of State for the Department of Industry) that approval had been given to restart the BAe 146 programme, the cost being estimated at £250 million, which was to be financed by the new nationalised company. British Aerospace at Hatfield began to build up the workforce, renegotiating contracts with original suppliers or finding new ones; this resulted in a risk-sharing contract with Avco Aerostructures in the USA to build the wings, providing a very high American value content with the engines, making the aircraft more attractive in the North American market.

At the time of the relaunch, the potential market was for a jet airliner on low-density routes of 150 to 350 miles from unsophisticated airports often located in demanding locations with short unmetaled runways and challenging obstacle clearance, or city centre airports where noise would be critical. The higher performance 146-100 would be able to carry up to eighty-five passengers, replacing the slower, smaller, twin prop-jet local service airliners, while the 146-200 could carry up to 100 passengers from less demanding airports. A market was estimated at some 1,500

BAe 146 nose assembly in the Erecting Shop on 12 May 1980 where Mosquitos, Comets, and Tridents had been built. (*BAe Photo*)

Early BAe 146 assembly in the Erecting Shop, 7 January 1981. (*BAe Photo*)

seventy–100-seat replacement airliners over the next decade, with the BAe 146 share at 400 aircraft and a break-even at 250, particularly if there was success with North American regional operators. In the event, the sales prediction proved unrealistic as the regional operators were unable to finance large batches of aircraft but could follow initial orders with regular repeat orders.

On 20 May 1981, when the first aircraft was rolled out, the long-awaited launch order was announced from US regional Air Wisconsin for four 146-200s, with options on four more, the 200 Series later becoming the best-selling version of the BAe 146. Further orders followed from the USA, the Series 100 attracting more of a niche market. Following the roll-out from the production line known as the Erecting Shop, the first aircraft (G-SSSH) was prepared for the flight development programme with a lengthy period of ground testing the systems, leading to first engine runs on 12 August 1981. When completed, the first aircraft had taxi runs and short hops by Mike Goodfellow (the chief test pilot) on 2 September, followed the next day by the ninety-five-minute maiden flight. The test fleet consisted of five aircraft, with Series 100 G-SSSH allocated to general handling, stalling, flutter, autopilot development, and CAA assessment.

The second 146-100 G-SSHH was used for power plant development, systems testing, and cold and hot weather trials. Series 100 G-SSCH was used for performance development, avionics testing, and noise measurement. The first 146-200 G-WISC in Air Wisconsin colours flew on 1 August 1982 and was used for Series 200 testing and American FAA certification, although it was never delivered to the airline. Finally, Series 100 G-OBAF in British Air Ferries colours was used on route proving. After some 1,500 hours of flight testing, British CAA certification was achieved on 4 February 1983, as the first type to be approved to the European Joint Airworthiness requirements. American FAA approval was awarded on 20 May 1983. By this time, there were modest orders for fourteen aircraft with options on a further sixteen, the initial British operator being Dan-Air for Series 100s, the first new aircraft to serve with the airline.

The first major development was the stretched fuselage BAe 146-300 when the original prototype was moved into Technical Services at Hatfield after its last flight on 7 August 1986, and the fuselage was cut into three sections. Details were revealed at the 1984 Farnborough Air Show, and there was an 8-foot 1-inch plug forward of the wing and 7 feet 8 inches aft, making the Series 300 8 feet longer than the 146-200. This increased passenger capacity to 100 five abreast or 112 six abreast with structural strengthening in the fuselage and top wing skins. A new cabin interior was introduced with larger luggage stowage, while the power plants remained the same 7,000-lb thrust ALF502R-5s.

BAe 146 G-ASSH was flown from Hatfield for the first time on 3 September 1981 by Mike Goodfellow and Peter Sedgewick. (*BAe Photo*)

First BAe 146-200 G-WISC in the colours of launch customer Air Wisconsin, which was retained by BAe and never delivered. (*BAe Photo*)

The completed conversion was backed out of Tech. Services on 8 March 1987 with the maiden flight deadline set by general manager Charles Masefield of noon on 1 May painted on the hangar door. The aircraft was fully repainted and registered G-LUXE; it was placed in a darkened new assembly hall next to the flight test hangar for the launch ceremony. As a Welsh male voice choir sang 'The Sound of Silence', the curtain was pulled back, the doors opened, and the aircraft rolled out ready to make its first flight by chief test pilot Peter Sedgewick in its new configuration at noon in front of 5,000 invited guests and employees, on schedule.

On the same day, a launch order was announced for five Series 300s by Air Wisconsin to add to the ten 146-200s already in service. After some 300 hours of flight development, certification was achieved on 6 September 1988 at the Farnborough Air Show where it was displayed, together with the former G-SSHH (which had been modified as a military transport as G-BSTA). The first production Series 300, registered G-OAJF after Tony Fairbrother (the Series 300 project manager), flew with an Electronic Flight Instrument System (EFIS) flight deck, which became standard on all BAe 146s the following year.

The first delivery was 146-100 G-BKMN to Dan-Air on 23 May 1983; four days later, it entered service from Gatwick to Dublin, going on to average eight and a half hours every day with a high level of reliability. It was soon joined by G-BKHT. A third 146-100 joined the airline in July 1984, later to be replaced by five longer 146-300s delivered from 1989 to 1992, although the airline went into liquidation in 1992. Other British operators were Stansted-based Air UK, Debonair low-cost airline from Luton, and Exeter-based British European (later to become Flybe).

With Air Wisconsin the launch customer for both the 146-200 and 146-300, the first delivery was 146-200 N601AW on 16 June 1983 entering service as a franchise partner to United Airlines. The new type replaced propeller-driven Dash 7s on a demanding thirteen daily sectors, the fleet eventually growing to fifteen aircraft by 1989. Other American operators were Pacific Southwest Airlines (PSA), Air Cal, Westair, Aspen, and Presidential, most of which were later merged into United Express.

In Canada, two regional airlines (Air BC and Air Nova) ordered a total of ten 146-200s feeding into Air Canada routes. The Antipodes was a popular region for BAe 146s with Ansett Australia, Australian Air Link—later to become part of Qantas and then Cobham as customers, while Ansett New Zealand ordered four 146-200s and later eight Series 300s. CAAC of China followed their Trident operations with an order for ten 146-100s and eight Series 300s. An order for two 146-100s came from Druk Air of Bhutan in the Himalayas, where it was the only jet airliner capable of operating from the mountain-surrounded Paro Airport, some

BAe 146-300 prototype G-LUXE being towed out from the new assembly hall ready for its first flight on 1 May 1987. (*Author's collection*)

BAe 146 production in the new assembly hall at Hatfield. (*BAe Photo*)

Handover of first customer BAe 146-100 (G-BKMN) to Dan-Air in the flight test hangar on 23 May 1983. (*BAe Photo*)

7,300 feet above sea level, VFR only. The author was fortunate to be able to visit the Kingdom of Bhutan, where the main diet is rice, the main export is hydroelectricity to India, and life expectancy is forty-five years. A mainline operator in Asia, Thai Airways, ordered a total of twelve BAe 146s, including one Series 100, eventually settling on a fleet of five Series 300s for domestic routes.

The flexibility in the BAe 146 design opened up a whole range of new roles, the first being the 'Quiet Trader'. Of particular advantage was the quietness of the fan engines, allowing overnight operations without restrictions. The high-wing, large unobstructed cabin and fuselage floor at truck-bed height made the fitting of a rear-fuselage upward-opening cargo door practical for overnight package flights. Both the Series 200 and 300 were offered, with the first aircraft for conversion leaving Hatfield in March 1986 to Hayes International at Dothan, Alabama, USA, returning five months later as N146QT.

Following a European demonstration, TNT bought the first conversion, followed by two more, with the first (G-TNTA) entering service in May 1987 based at the Cologne Airport hub. The author experienced overnight package sorties in G-TNTB from Luton to Nuremberg, Cologne/Bonn, and back to Luton in June 1988 with a flight time of three hours and five

Annual Hatfield Open Day in July 1986 with Air Cal BAe 146-200 N146AC and BAe 125-700 G-BFAN on static display. (*Author's collection*)

minutes. In June 1988, TNT expressed a commitment for every 146QT built over the next five years, totalling seventy-two aircraft, allowing a global expansion in TNT's overnight cargo network. However, there was strong competition from Boeing and McDonnell Douglas for lower-priced conversions of hush-kitted 737s and MD-80s despite their higher noise levels; although BAe agreed to build the 146QTs at cost, TNT only took twenty-one aircraft, with seven going to other operators.

The size of the initial TNT commitment prompted the opening of another assembly line at Woodford to accelerate overall production to forty aircraft per year in the vast assembly hall where Avro had built Lancaster and Vulcan bombers. This complemented the £4 million invested in the new assembly hall at Hatfield, which could accommodate four BAe 146s at a time surrounded by staging for efficient final assembly and equipping with systems and interiors. Using the cargo door modifications with the 146QT allowed a quiet convertible to be produced in a mixed passenger/cargo configuration, but only five were built.

Following previous de Havilland aircraft serving as royal flight transports, in the spring of 1983, two BAE 146-100s were purchased for evaluation for the Queen's Flight to replace earlier HS 748s. Prince Philip had already flown the type, and two CC Mk 1s (ZD695 and ZD696) were issued to 10 Squadron at Brize Norton for an evaluation of about a year.

TNT 146QT Quiet Trader during overnight operations at Nuremburg, 10 June 1988. (*Author's collection*)

Following this evaluation, two new Series 100s were ordered as CC Mk 2s with additional wing-root fuel tanks, giving a range of 1,700 miles. The two aircraft were handed over after fitting out at Broughton in April and July 1986; they were joined by a third in December 1990, but the latter was withdrawn from use at the end of 2001.

In 1995, the Queen's Flight was moved from Benson and amalgamated with 32 Squadron at Northolt to become 32 (The Royal) Squadron, providing VIP transport not just for the Royal Family, but also for Government Ministers and military VIPs. It now has additional BAe 146s to cover its expanded task of Command Support Air Transport, having supplied logistics support for military operations in the turbulent Middle East. In June 2012, BAE Systems was awarded a contract to convert two Series 200 QCs to military configuration to compliment RAF tactical aircraft during the withdrawal from Afghanistan in 2013–14, the new version being designated C Mk 3 and retained the cargo door in the rear cabin, with seating for up to ninety-four passengers. The first of the two (ZE707) was delivered in February 2013, arriving in Kandahar on 22 February, where it was badly damaged by a violent hailstorm, later to be repaired.

During the late 1980s, there was a steady demand for smaller airliners, with many of the existing BAe 146 customers undercapitalised and therefore unable to finance orders for new airliners. The major lease companies had not adopted the BAe 146 programme, resulting in a serious financial exposure to British Aerospace in backing production efforts with not only the 146, but also Woodford's ATP and Prestwick's Jetstream. BAe was forced to sell the aircraft to finance companies, which then leased the aircraft back to British Aerospace, to then pass them on to the operators on short flexible subleases, while the manufacturer arranged a head lease for fifteen to eighteen years.

Deregulation of the American airline industry resulted in the creation of many start-up airlines with minimal financial backing. The company strategy appeared to work until 1992, when the plummeting global economy caused a major reduction in business for airlines, and significant numbers of aircraft were returned off lease at much-reduced values. There was little chance of establishing new operators at sustainable rates, resulting in BAe being responsible for continued payments to finance companies, with British Aerospace coming close to insolvency.

Faced with this situation, the company completed a major restructure of the regional aircraft business, making a special provision in the accounts of £1 billion. Reserves were virtually wiped out with the company net worth reduced to £1.7 billion, only £100 million above the lower limit set by the company's banking covenants. The regional aircraft business had been driven by the need to keep the factories busy, not achieving a reasonable return on investment. British Aerospace had in effect become a bank guarantor for a number of underfinanced start-up airlines, with returned aircraft becoming a financial burden to the company. It was better to sell to established airlines even at a lower cost, to generate cash and a better yield. Production rate was reduced dramatically from forty-two aircraft a year to between eighteen and twenty, the rate being market-driven.

To cope with the large fleet of BAe 146s, ATPs, and Jetstreams, in January 1993, Asset Management was formed at the new Bishop's Square development on the aerodrome boundary near the Comet Hotel, to manage this large fleet of out-of-service aircraft. The situation was stabilised quickly, with BAe responsible for new aircraft sales of what was the RJs (short for regional jets) on the Woodford production line. When Asset Management started, there were 118 BAe 146s on the books, with twenty-one stored and another forty due to be returned in 1993, with forty-four idle at the peak of the recession.

Within three years, Asset Management had reduced to stored fleet to zero and had raised the market value to help support the production of new aircraft. Asset management later became Falko with a responsibility of managing the regional aircraft fleet, including a number being parted out for spares recovery, and at the end of 2017, they had disposed of their last BAe 146 on the books, but they continue in business, managing other airliners, including Boeing types.

During the 1980s, productivity at Hatfield continued to improve with a high level of co-operation from all levels of the workforce, where the de Havilland ethos still existed. However, it was clear that British Aerospace strategy was to dispose of its factories and airfields in the south of Britain to reduce costs and raise funds to continue to develop the business. The factory at Hurn was closed in 1983, followed by Weybridge/Brooklands in 1987 and Kingston in 1992, the latter two being long-established and pioneering sites in British aviation.

Hatfield was no exception as it was worth more in the short term for development than transforming basic materials into a world-beating product earning valuable foreign currency. However, continued investment was high, and it was announced in March 1991 that 146 assembly would be concentrated at Woodford, with the last aircraft completed at Hatfield (146-200 G-ISEE) making its first flight on 23 March 1992. Productivity still continued to improve, but the end was near and work transferred out with the aerodrome closing on 4 April 1994. There had been plans to retain the airfield by Hatfield Business Aviation already established at the old flying school building, but the last flight was organised by the Moth Club; however, this was limited due to high winds to Tiger Moth G-APLU, flown by Dick Bishop (son of R. E. Bishop, the Mosquito and Comet designer) and carrying Ann Essex (the founder's granddaughter) as a passenger.

The factory went into a level of dereliction while plans were made for its development, but it was resuscitated for the Tom Hanks movie *Saving Private Ryan*, when Steven Speilberg used the board room as his office, and the factory was used to build the sets, including a town with a bridge across a river. After the movie, the runway where so many aircraft had taken off and landed was broken up, with a section of the perimeter track remaining in the green belt-designated area on the western half of the former airfield. The main administration building on the Barnet Bypass was Grade II listed, not just for its 1930s Art Deco design, but also with the board room as the location of so many major pioneering decisions. Also listed was the adjacent works canteen and restaurant with its sprung upper ballroom floor, and the gatehouse now separated from the old personnel department, which has become a KFC restaurant.

The other main evidence of de Havilland's origins is the Grade II*-listed flight test hangar, which is now a fitness centre. A condition of the use as a fitness centre is that no changes are made to the structure, and the hangar doors are operational, although the western end has been folded back and encapsulated with a new wall across. There is also a heritage walk around the commercial site, starting at the University of Hertfordshire Campus.

BAe Commercial Aircraft Division, Hatfield, with Bishop's Square in the lower centre, which was to replace the original design building. Behind the new assembly hall is the flight test hangar and beyond is the main factory. (*BAe Photo*)

Sub-assembly department at Hatfield where BAe 146 components were built, including undercarriage and cabin doors. (*BAe Photo*)

Hatfield Business Aviation with visiting business jets outside the old flying school. (*Author's collection*)

With the closure of Hatfield, many of the otherwise redundant employees were invited to move to the Woodford area, particularly from the design team and other specialist departments. The move was followed by the launch of the RJ family with a more reliable and powerful ALF 507, new flight deck avionics (including Cat 3A autoland), increases in payload, capacity, and range, and improved interior transforming the BAe 146 from a local service airliner in an unsophisticated environment, into a main-line regional jet. The new family became the RJ70, RJ85, and RJ100 (based on the 146 Series 100, Series 200, and Series 300 respectively) with the same nominal seat count.

Three aircraft were allocated to the flight test programme at Woodford representing the three variants. Joint airworthiness approval was achieved for the RJ85 in March 1993, followed by RJ100 in July and RJ70 in August, followed by FAA approval in September. The new types were then rebranded as Avro RJs and the first customer delivery was to Crossair of Switzerland, followed by Lufthansa, Sabena, and British Airways.

Another major operator was THY of Turkey who ordered a total of ten RJ100s and four RJ70s for domestic and international services. The largest single order for RJs was from Sabena who signed for twenty-three RJ85s in September 1995, to be used by Delta Air Transport, who was already an operator of six 146-200s. Unfortunately, following 9/11, Sabena went into liquidation on 6 November 2001, but some aircraft continued to be flown by independent SN Brussels. British Airways used their regional subsidiary City Express to operate the RJs. A major American operator was Northwest, with thirty-six RJ85s between 1997 and 2000, but it went into liquidation in 2006, many of its fleet going into service with Dublin based CityJet. BAe 146s and RJs were major users of London City Airport, leading to the success of the City air gateway.

Further improvements were developed at Woodford in what became to be known as the Avro RJX, which included increased range, with new Honeywell AS977 turbofans with reduced fuel burn and maintenance costs to be developed in the typical three different versions. With the merger of British Aerospace and Marconi Electronic Systems in November 1999, the new company became BAE Systems. In March 2000, the Avro RJX was launched as a low-cost, low-risk, high-gain development programme, with a very competitive low acquisition cost, the first RJX development aircraft making its first flight from Woodford on 28 April 2001, followed by RJ100 on 23 September. The launch customer was Druk Air, who ordered a pair of RJ85s for the demanding operation into Paro, and BA franchise partner CityFlyer Express placed six options for RJX100s, followed by British European ordering 12 RJX100s. Development flying continued with the two initial aircraft, but the effects of 9/11 had global economic results severely depressing air travel.

On 27 November 2001, BAE Systems chief executive, John Weston made a shock and unexpected announcement. Due to the severe downturn in the commercial aerospace market following 9/11, the regional jet airliner business was no longer viable, causing the cancellation of the RJX programme. By this time, there was also growing competition from the regional jets produced by Brazil's Embraer and Canadian Bombardier, resulting in the more sophisticated RJX being overpriced for the market. The flight development programme was to continue to satisfy the outstanding orders from Druk Air and British European, with the aircraft to be built if the airlines still wanted them, although keeping a production line open for five years to deliver twelve aircraft to British European was hardly practical. In January 2002, BAE Systems announced that neither airline would be taking their aircraft, with flying stopping immediately and the airlines paid compensation. Only three RJXs flew and the last flight was by G-IRJX for preservation at Manchester Airport on 16 February 2003, where it is part of the air transport collection at the viewing area.

The final British jet airliner (RJ85 OH-SAP) was delivered to Finish Blue 1 on 26 November 2003, ending twenty-two years of BAe 146/RJ airliner production. The last airliner in the vast Woodford assembly hall was the original BAe 146-100 prototype, converted to the prototype Series 300 G-LUXE, which had been used at Woodford for icing trials with later LF507 engines. It was then converted on the production line as an atmospheric research aircraft with the structure zero life, ready for delivery from Woodford to Cranfield on 10 May 2004 to be operated by the Facility for Airborne Atmospheric Measurements (FAAM).

Woodford continued as the base for the development and production of Nimrod MR 4 maritime reconnaissance aircraft for the RAF, although flight testing was based at Warton. In the Conservative Strategic Defence and Security Review, due to massive cost overruns and delays in service entry, the government announced the cancellation of the programme on 19 October 2010, and the site closed on 25 August 2011 to be developed for housing. With the closure and demolition of the factory, type design approval for the BAe 146 was moved to BAE Systems at Prestwick, where it remains, supporting a global fleet, including the aircraft being converted to air tankers for the very effective fire fighting role, particularly in the USA and Australia.

Further Reading

Birtles P. J., *de Havilland Comet* (Shepperton: Ian Allan, 1990)

Birtles P. J., *de Havilland Mosquito: The Original Multirole Combat Aircraft* (Fonthill Media, 2015)

Birtles P. J., *de Havilland Vampire, Venom and Sea Vixen* (Shepperton: Ian Allan, 1986)

Gunston B., *Hawker: The Story of the 125* (Airworthy Publications)

Jackson A. J., *de Havilland Aircraft Since 1909* (London: Putnam, 1987)

Martin C. H., *de Havilland Blue Streak* (London: British Interplanetary Society)

Sharp C. M., *D H An Outline of de Havilland History* (London: Faber & Faber, 1960)

Skinner S., *BAe 146: Britain's Best Selling Jet Airliner* (Stamford: Key Publishing)

Skinner S., *Classic Airliner: The Hawker Siddeley Trident* (Stamford: Key Publishing)